P9-DDV-627

RICHLER

THE APPRENTICESHIP OF DUDDY KRAVITZ

AND OTHER WORKS

NOTES

COLES EDITORIAL BOARD

Bound to stay open

Publisher's Note

Otabind (Ota-bind). This book has been bound using the patented Otabind process. You can open this book at any page, gently run your finger down the spine, and the pages will lie flat.

ABOUT COLES NOTES

COLES NOTES have been an indispensible aid to students on five continents since 1948.

COLES NOTES are available for a wide range of individual literary works. Clear, concise explanations and insights are provided along with interesting interpretations and evaluations.

Proper use of COLES NOTES will allow the student to pay greater attention to lectures and spend less time taking notes. This will result in a broader understanding of the work being studied and will free the student for increased participation in discussions.

COLES NOTES are an invaluable aid for review and exam preparation as well as an invitation to explore different interpretive paths.

COLES NOTES are written by experts in their fields. It should be noted that any literary judgement expressed herein is just that — the judgement of one school of thought. Interpretations that diverge from, or totally disagree with any criticism may be equally valid.

COLES NOTES are designed to supplement the text and are not intended as a substitute for reading the text itself. Use of the NOTES will serve not only to clarify the work being studied, but should enhance the reader's enjoyment of the topic.

ISBN 0-7740-3278-2

© COPYRIGHT 1994 AND PUBLISHED BY
COLES PUBLISHING COMPANY
TORONTO—CANADA
PRINTED IN CANADA

Manufactured by Webcom Limited
Cover finish: Webcom's Exclusive **Duracoat**

' . . . I'm a failure. All I needed was to be born rich. All I needed was money in the crib and I would have grown up such a fine, lovable guy. A kidder. A regular prince among men. God damn it to hell, he thought, why was I born the son of a dope?'

(p. 298–299)

CONTENTS

THE AUTHOR

In "The Uncertain World", an essay written for *Canadian Literature* (No. 41, Summer 1969), Mordecai Richler points with mock pride at his accomplishments as a writer and quotes the *Oxford Companion to Canadian Literature* as evidence that he has not been unsuccessful:

> Richler, Mordecai (1931) Born in Montreal, he was educated at Sir George Williams College and spent two years abroad. Returning to Canada in 1952, he joined the staff of the Canadian Broadcasting Corporation. He now lives in England, where he writes film scripts, novels, and short stories.

In part, of course, Richler is lampooning the kind of dull notation which passes for autobiographical information in encyclopaedias and reference books. In part, also, however, he is making the point that there is much to his story as a man and as a writer that such a note fails to recognize. The observation is a just one and is delivered with Richler's characteristic puckish humour.

Mordecai Richler was born in 1931 in the ghetto world of Jewish Montreal. It takes little imagination to picture the environment into which he was thrust, for it is vividly portrayed in *The Apprenticeship of Duddy Kravitz:*

> To a middle-class stranger, it's true, one street would have seemed as squalid as the next. On each corner a cigar store, a grocery, and a fruit man. Outside staircases everywhere. Winding ones, wooden ones, rusty and risky ones. Here a prized plot of grass splendidly barbered, there a spitefully weedy patch. An endless repetition of precious peeling balconies and waste lots making the occasional gap here and there.
>
> (p. 13)*

It may have seemed squalid to an outsider, yet in a sense it was a world of dreams and aspirations. It was, as it were, the mid-point between two other Jewish worlds: one, the much poorer streets south of St. Lawrence; the other, Outremont, to which the more successful Jews moved. In its own way, then, Richler's environment was a strange mixture of dream and reality, which helps to explain

---

* All page references in these notes to *The Apprenticeship of Duddy Kravitz* refer to the Penguin Books edition (1964).

his statement, quoted by George Woodcock in the introduction to *Son of a Smaller Hero,* that "the ghetto of Montreal has no real walls and no true dimensions. The walls are the habit of atavism and the dimensions are an illusion. But the ghetto exists all the same." Without doubt, Richler's environment also helps us to understand the world of *Duddy Kravitz*. Dreams dominate in the novel. The old men, suffocated by their ugly environment, dream of land:

> . . . Sitting in their dark cramped ghetto corners they wrote the most mawkish, school-girlish stuff about green fields and sky. Terrible poetry, but touching when you consider the circumstances under which it was written.

> (p. 310)

Similarly, the Boy Wonder, in spite of the criminal and inhuman source of his wealth, provides a dream of escape. And the grandest dream of all is that of Duddy's passion to become something more than an insignificant ghetto boy.

Richler's early years conformed to a common pattern. His father was a junk dealer, and Mordecai had the usual spate of part-time jobs. However, when he was thirteen his parents divorced, and the event seems to have caused some change in direction. Until that time, Mordecai had been orthodox in faith and had attended the Jewish parochial school. Afterwards he lapsed from orthodoxy. This change is probably an important clue to the satirical element in Richler's work, for he has the gift, so necessary in the satirist, of combining compassionate understanding and merciless objectivity. Thus he is able to point out the faults of the people from whom he sprang because, in the words of his mother, he "loves them so much."

After parochial school, Richler attended Baron Byng High School, which appears as Fletcher's Field in *Duddy Kravitz*. The novel probably gives a fair picture of Baron Byng, for the teachers were largely Anglo-Saxon, with little obvious sympathy for their Jewish charges. Certainly, like Duddy, Richler did not distinguish himself scholastically, though he does admit in *The Streets* "I must say we were not a promising or engaging bunch. We were scruffy and spiteful, with an eye on the main chance." Whatever the reason, Richler's marks were too low to enable him to enter McGill University. He was obliged to proceed instead to Sir George Williams College, a small college at that time and largely devoted to students unable to meet the stiff entrance requirements elsewhere.

Richler has described the college as "sort of a loser's finishing school." In any case, he did not stay long enough at Sir George Williams to graduate. One reason for that may have been his instinctive suspicion of the academic life, which he has described pungently in *The Uncertain World*s

> All of us tend to romanticize the world we nearly chose. In my case, academe, where, like all good spellers on tenure, I would own a Ph.D. Instead of having to bring home the meat, I would only be obliged to stamp it, rejecting this shoulder of beef as Hank James derivative, that side of pork as sub-Jimmy Joyce. I saw myself as no longer a perplexed free-lancer with an unpredictable income, balancing this magazine assignment, that film job, against the time it would buy me. No sir. Sipping Tio Pepe in the faculty club, snug in my leather wing-backed chair, in the cherished company of other disinterested scholars, speculating on the significance of the comparable Frederick Philip Grove. I would not, given the assurance of a monthly cheque, chat about anything so coarse as money.

Undoubtedly, however, this suspicion was generated by his main desire, which was to become a writer. Thus he felt that were he to involve himself in strictly academic pursuits and scholastic endeavours, his urge to write might be deadened. Certainly writing was his principal objective, for one acquaintance declared: "The thing I remember is that there was nothing tentative about his desire to become a writer. He said 'I am going to become a writer' and that was that."

Consequently, in 1951, financed by an insurance policy which he had cashed, Richler left behind the academic world of Sir George Williams and the Jewish world of Montreal and journeyed to Paris. It was, in many ways, the same kind of pilgrimage that English, American and Canadian writers had made in the thirties, when Paris had been the intellectual oasis for aspiring writers and painters whose genius had not yet been recognized by their homelands. Scott Fitzgerald and Ernest Hemingway were in those earlier days two prominent inhabitants of the city's left bank; Canada's Morley Callaghan had been a friend of both Fitzgerald and Hemingway in Paris; and T. S. Eliot had also sojourned in Paris. In the 1950's the names of the creative emigrés had changed – Terry Southern, Mavis Gallant, Allen Ginsberg – but the nature of the stimulus had not. Paris, through the works of French writers such as Camus and Sartre, was still the intellectual heart of Europe, particularly with regard to existentialist philosophy, which in the postwar years spread from Europe and found expression in the works of such different writers as Saul Bellow, Samuel Beckett and Arthur Koestler. In Paris, Richler adopted the life style of the cultural emigrés. Short of money, he lived poorly, yet still managed to visit Spain and also England, where he met E. M. Forster briefly. He wrote steadily, but his work was not published except in a little magazine.

Still without money, Richler returned to Canada after two years. However, he now had something tangible and significant, the manuscript for a novel, which he left with an agent in London on his way to Montreal. The novel, *The Acrobats,* was published in 1954 and, after the style of Hemingway, told of the life and death in Spain of a young Canadian artist. The book received some praise in London, but was largely ignored in Canada. The lukewarm reception accorded the novel is probably due in large measure to its derivative nature, for, as George Bowering pointed out, "Richler sometimes seems to sacrifice his art to a love-hate attitude to Hemingway's works, especially to *For Whom the Bell Tolls.*" Thus, though Bowering writes sympathetically, he has seen clearly the major fault:

> But this is Richler's first book, and as often happens in first books, the young author's literary ghosts are difficult to allay. So that later, when Andre is preparing in his drunkenness to poke his fist at the Nazi Kraus, Richler sees him through the literary trick (Hemingway's word) that comes via Hemingway's "Up in Michigan" from the advice of Gertrude Stein:
>
> > Andre laughed. He laughed and laughed and laughed. He laughed because Chaim was a useful man and he laughed because Kraus was a brute. He clutched the banister and doubled up laughing. He laughed because Ida was dead and he laughed because probably he did not love Toni. He laughed because he was drunk. He laughed and laughed. He laughed because he was feverish and he laughed because the doctors said he would go mad. Tears rolled down his cheeks, and he laughed.
>
> All the directionless bar scenes of *The Acrobats* are like expatriate *The Sun Also Rises* scenes, but without even the desperate gaiety of the Jake Barnes crowd – rather with a soft and aimless self-hate.
>
> (*Canadian Literature*, No. 29, Summer 1966)

Whatever the critical reception, there can be no doubt of Richler's own reaction to publication of the novel. Writing eighteen years later, he commented:

> . . . There is nothing I cherish so much as the first and most vulnerable book, *The Acrobats,* published in 1954, not only because it marked the first time my name appeared in a Canadian newspaper, a prescient Toronto columnist writing from London, "You've not heard of Mordecai Richler yet, but, look out, she's a name to watch

for"; but also because it was the one book I could write as a totally private act, with the deep, inner assurance that nobody would be such a damn fool as to publish it. That any editor would boot it back to me, a condescending rejection note enclosed, enabling me to quit Paris for Montreal, an honourable failure, and get down to the serious business of looking for a job. A real job.

Don't blame me, but André Deutsch. To my astonishment (and I say this without false modesty), the novel was published in England and the U.S., and translated into five languages. Now, when somebody asked me what I did, I could reply, without seeming fraudulent to myself, that I was indeed a writer.

The key sentence in that statement is the last one, for the publication of his first novel decided the course of Richler's aspirations. He moved to London in 1954 and devoted himself to writing. In 1955, his second novel, *Son of a Smaller Hero,* appeared. In this book Richler left behind the Europe of the existentialists and wrote of the world he knew intimately, the Jewish ghetto of Montreal. Though Donald Cameron has dismissed the book as "a crisp and ironic Portrait of the Artist as a Poor Kid in Montreal," *Son of a Smaller Hero* is significant in that it shows that Richler had found the locale in which he was to be most successful. Indeed, so successful was he in recreating that world of St. Lawrence Boulevard that he had to add a warning note:

Although all the streets described in this book are real streets, and the seasons, tempers and moods are those of Montreal as I remember them, all the characters portrayed are works of the imagination and all the situations they find themselves in are fictional. Any reader approaching this book in a search for "real people" is completely on the wrong track and, what's more, has misunderstood my whole purpose. *Son of a Smaller Hero* is a novel, not an autobiography.

Though, then, the novel was something of a scandal among the Jewish community of Montreal, where there was a hunt to "identify" characters, *Son of a Smaller Hero* marks in a modest way the first vivid signs of Richler's ability to portray the universal through the particular. He selected what he knew well and wrote of it with such shrewdness and insight that it became more than a local portrait. George Woodcock has discerned that gift precisely:

Son of a Smaller Hero is, in its narrowest sense, the account of an attempt by a Jewish youth in Montreal to escape from the mental bonds of the ghetto, and, having passed through the feared and desired world of the *Goyim,* to realize his true self in the freedom which he believes exists beyond the invisible walls. Turning by turning, the vistas open. The little border territory in which Noah Adler's experiences are developed becomes the microcosm of a whole city, and, by the multiplication of the reflections, the microcosm of a whole country that lives by the mutual attractions of the divided.

For his fourth novel, *The Apprenticeship of Duddy Kravitz,* published in 1959, Richler returned to Montreal for his setting. *Duddy Kravitz* was a critical success, but a financial failure. *Time* magazine has described it as "the book that established the author's literary voice." Certainly, the talent which Woodcock saluted in *Son of a Smaller Hero* is even more plainly evident in *Duddy Kravitz*. Under Richler's craftsmanship the narrative was not simply the struggle of a poor young Jew to do well in a hostile environment that spurned his dreams. The story that Richler fashioned was much more archetypal, evoking echoes of the experience of Huckleberry Finn in his initiation into manhood on the Mississippi River. *Duddy Kravitz* does, it is true, comment satirically on many aspects of life in Montreal; it does deal in some way with the problem of Jew and Gentile relationships, a problem that is felt acutely by some in Montreal; and it is a kind of *exposé* of such things as the curse of materialism and the hypocrisy of urban dwellers. However, Richler's Duddy became, not simply a Jew encountering specific setbacks and difficulties, but, more than that, a microcosm of the young man agonizingly seeking his identity and his place in society. Thus the year 1959 was significant in the career of Mordecai Richler because in that year *Duddy Kravitz* proved beyond doubt Richler's ability to speak not just to French Canadians or English Canadians or Jewish Canadians or to any Canadians in particular, but to a universal audience of men who could respond sympathetically to the author's expression of the pathos and irony inherent in all human existence. This is why *Time* could declare that *Duddy Kravitz* was "the book that established the author's literary voice." Richler had left behind imitative styles and themes and had broadened the concerns of *Son of a Smaller Hero* into larger human concerns.

Within a span of six years, Richler had now published four novels. He had established himself as a writer. He engaged in his vocation prolifically and enthusiastically. He wrote film scripts and he wrote numerous articles for magazines of all kinds. Indeed, many Canadians probably know Richler only as a writer for magazines. Naturally, being a well-known Canadian living in London, Richler's articles often dealt pungently with things Canadian. His witty and satirical observations have, of course, brought sharp criticism. Thus Donald Cameron (*The Canadian Forum,* March 1972) viewed Richler's journalism with something less than enthusiasm:

"Being a Canadian writer abroad offers a number of useful perks," Richler confessed four years ago, in *The New York Review*. "I have over the years, been turning over a useful penny in the why-have-you-left-Canada interview." A useful penny is altogether too modest. As one leading Canadian editor says, "Mordecai has really built a thriving cottage industry out of knocking Canada."

But "after thirteen almost uninterrupted years abroad," Richler conceded in the same essay, "I no longer understood the idiom. Doomed to always be a foreigner in England, I was now in danger of finding Canada foreign too." Never mind: mere ignorance never prevents a real pro from turning a Useful Penny. Articles continued to stream from our self-appointed interpreter to the world, the Just Add Hot Water and Serve expert on Canada.

Such criticism of Richler's prolific journalism is not uncommon. By setting himself up as Canada's gadfly, he has certainly laid himself open to the charge of artistic commercialism. This complaint is at the root of Morley Callaghan's observation: "His weakness is that he'll write you a piece about anything, any time, at the drop of a hat. Well, it's a question of how often you can do that sort of thing." Nor are the critics silenced by Richler's own attitude to his varied assignments. Talking humorously about the "useful perks" of being a Canadian writer abroad or about "turning over a useful penny in the why-have-you-left-Canada interview" hardly soothes ruffled critical feathers.

Nevertheless, it is essential to bear in mind Richler's own sense of dedication to his main task, that of being a writer. The journalism is mere froth, in a real sense only one of the "useful perks." The real vocation is evident in *The Uncertain World* where, following the example of George Orwell, Richler has given four reasons why he wants to write:

(1) . . . egoism informed by imagination, style, and a desire to be known, yes, *but only on your own conditions*.

(2) Like any serious writer, I desperately want to write one novel that will last, something that will make me remembered after death, and so I am compelled to keep trying.

(3) "Historical impulse. Desire to see things as they are." No matter how long I continue to live abroad, I do feel forever rooted in St. Urbain Street. This was my time, my place, and I have elected myself to get it exactly right.

(4) "Political purpose – using the word 'political' in the widest possible sense. Desire to push the world in a certain direction, to alter other people's idea of the kind of society that they should strive after."

   Not an overlarge consideration in my work, though I would say that any serious writer is a moralist, and only incidentally an entertainer.

The Apprenticeship of Duddy Kravitz was adapted to the screen and became a commercial success. More recently, a musical stage production of the book revived the novel.

Richler's fifth novel, *The Incomparable Atuk* (1963) was followed by *Cocksure* in 1968 and *Tigers Under Glass* in the same year. *The Street* appeared in 1969 and in 1971 *St. Urbain's Horseman* was published. *Shovelling Trouble* (1972) was followed by *Jacob Two-Two Meets the Hooded Fang* (1975), *A Choice of Enemies* (1977), *The Great Comic Book Heroes and Other Essays* (1978), *Joshua Then and Now* (1981), *The Best of Modern Humour* and *Essays on Canada* (edited by Richler in 1983), and the novel *Home Sweet Home* in 1984.

Mordecai Richler lived in England for many years, but, by his own confession, Canada in general and St. Urbain Street, (Montreal) in particular are inescapable facets of his experience. Richler currently resides in Montreal. As he said in an interview with the late Nathan Cohen, "All my attitudes are Canadian. I'm a Canadian; there's nothing to be done about it."

CHAPTER SUMMARIES AND COMMENTARIES

Part One

Chapter One

Summary

Feeling "unusually glum" because of his wife's illness and the prospect of three more days of teaching before the weekend, Mr. MacPherson made his way towards Fletcher's Field High School. On first arriving at the school, twenty years before, he had dreamed idealistically about his career; now, for some time he had "felt nothing about the building."

Both the school and Mr. MacPherson had changed with the years. Ten years hence, it would no longer be *the* Jewish high school; already there were three gentile students. Mr. MacPherson's face had become "more bitingly angry," and by 1947 he had become a heavy drinker. However, he had still not yet strapped anyone.

Mr. MacPherson encountered a group of students lounging against a shop window. Prominent among them was Duddy Kravitz, "a small, narrow-chested boy of fifteen," who was smoking a cigarette. The teacher was unwilling to reprimand the boys but felt obliged to do so, and ordered Duddy to put out the cigarette. Being informed that Duddy's father was aware of his son's smoking, Mr. MacPherson made the mistake of declaring that Mr. Kravitz was "not fit to bring up a boy." Leaving the boys, the teacher prepared to enter the school. As he did so, he was struck on the back of the neck by a snowball. He could not discover who was responsible. However, Duddy was the marksman.

Mr. MacPherson's class had the reputation of being the toughest in the school. His colleagues considered him too soft for the assignment, particularly since the burden of his wife's illness. When Mr. MacPherson entered his room, the boys were unusually quiet, but trouble was waiting. On the blackboard had been drawn "the chalk figure of a lean man being crushed by a snowball." Mr. MacPherson tried unsuccessfully to discover who was responsible for the caricature, but only succeeded in causing another confrontation with Duddy, who declared afterwards: "Mac is gonna wish he was never born." The boys had various methods for tormenting different teachers; Duddy was going to subject Mr. MacPherson to a spate of anonymous phone calls.

After school, the boys in Duddy's group wandered through the streets of the neighbourhood. On the way, Duddy told them fabulous stories of the exploits of his brother Bradley. They suspected that he was a fictional hero, but did not accuse Duddy of lying. Their reason for not doing so was simple: "Duddy was kind of funny, that's all." The group then noticed a Christian mission, with a neon sign outside proclaiming "Jesus Saves," in English and in Yiddish. The boys entered the little shop and teased the converted Jew who was in charge. They invited him to visit the high school during lunch hour to hand out his evangelical pamphlets to students. Afterwards, Duddy and his friends tormented the students of the rabbinical college by pelting them with pamphlets and snowballs. Marching off, the boys sang an obscene song.

Commentary

(1)   The opening chapter depicts vividly the major setting of the novel. We encouter the city of Montreal but, more important, the Jewish section of the city of Montreal. It is not a prosperous environment. Indeed, we are told that to a middle-class stranger "one street would have seemed as squalid as the next." Those Jews who achieved material success left the neighbourhood in order to "buy their own duplexes in the tree-lined streets of Outremont" (p. 7). Those who remained seemed to value money and popular acclaim, as suggested by the mention of the fabulous Jerry Dingleman and Duddy's stories of his brother (p. 14). In addition, there are signs of the erosion of the Jewish heritage. Fletcher's Field High School now had not only Anglo-Saxon students, but also Ukranians, Poles and Yugoslavs. In contrast, years before, most Jewish boys in Montreal who had been to high school had attended Fletcher's Field. Further, the treatment of the rabbinical students by Duddy and his friends hardly reveals an orthodox respect for religious tradition. Thus, while the tempo of the first chapter is undoubtedly satirical and humorous, we are nonetheless presented with the portrait of an environment which is suffering social and cultural change.

(2)   It is worth noting carefully the portrait of Mr. MacPherson in these pages. There can be little doubt that the dry, shrivelled, unhappy teacher acts as a foil for the ebullient and irreverent Duddy Kravitz. However, in addition, Mr. MacPherson almost seems to be

the image of the environment of the novel. His decline mirrors the decline of the school and may suggest the decline of the social environment.

(3)   The tone of the chapter sets the tone of the book, and that is accomplished by the presence of Duddy Kravitz. Mainly through the use of comic episodes, Richler has prepared the reader for the irreverent humour of what is to come. Duddy is resourceful, independent and elusive. These are all qualities which illuminate the rest of the book.

Chapter Two

Summary

After school, Mr. MacPherson decided to buy his wife, Jenny, a box of chocolates. However, first he visited the Pines Tavern. Thinking over the day's events, he concluded that he had been right to call Kravitz a coward, but he was apprehensive of the revenge his students might take. Nevertheless, no matter what happened, he would not use the strap. The principle behind not strapping was, like many of his dreams, dead, but it was still important to him not to strap. As long as he did not use the strap, he felt he would survive.

Arriving home, Mr. MacPherson realized that he had forgotten to buy the chocolates. There were also two visitors waiting: Herbert and Clara Shields. MacPherson and his wife were very uncomfortable, because Herbert Shields, who had been a McGill acquaintance, had achieved considerable material success in the pulp and paper business. MacPherson knew that the Shields considered him a failure, and he could imagine the comments they would make to their friends: "He's a failure, my dear, absolutely, and the Colby girl, the minister's daughter if you remember, well, she's turned out an invalid."

After the Shields left, MacPherson meant to work on his overdue history test papers, but he was too tired. Remembering wisely to unhook the phone, he and his wife went to bed. Jenny awoke at three in the morning with an acute pain. Realizing the futility of calling the doctor, who would only recommend once more an impossible holiday, MacPherson gave his wife sedatives and spent an anxious night watching over her in her sleep.

Commentary

(1)   The hopelessness of MacPherson's situation is emphasized. He is acutely aware himself of a sense of failure, as we see from his

encounter with the Shields and from his despair over his wife's illness. The incident of the forgotten chocolates underlines his deterioration, for he had spent his time drinking in the tavern, in spite of his real concern for Jenny.

(2) The pathos evoked by the situation of MacPherson is to offer sharp contrast with Duddy's life style. Duddy – and this will become even more apparent as the book proceeds – is not a sentimentalist. His treatment of MacPherson will, not uncharacteristically, seem to be cruel, ruthless and unfeeling.

(3) MacPherson's clinging tenaciously to his refusal to strap is, of course, an empty gesture. It is no more than a token acknowledgement that he once affirmed principles that were meaningful to him. Thus, the principle, and all the idealism and courage behind it, is dead; only the stubborn refusal to perform the action is left. In this way, MacPherson's affirmation is devoid of real significance. It becomes one of the common clichés of the novel mouthed by people such as Max and Duddy, revealing the pathetic emptiness at the heart of the characters.

Chapter Three

Summary

It was after seven o'clock when Duddy arrived home. His father was out, but his brother Lennie, a medical student, was in his bedroom studying anatomy. Duddy tried to tell Lennie about some of the day's events, but the brother was too busy. Lennie felt guilty about his treatment of Duddy and invited him to the movies on Saturday with Riva, Lennie's girlfriend. Duddy refused because he had been invited to a musical evening at the house of Mr. Cox.

Mr. Cox, the newest teacher in the school, was, in Duddy's opinion, "the World's No. 1 Crap-Artist," and his music was a bore. However, the boys enjoyed the hot dogs, the cokes and the laughs. They resisted Mrs. Cox's attempts to improve their language and discussed vigorously her sexuality. However, that night Duddy left early, angered by Mrs. Cox's suggestion that he flipped through books looking for the sexy passages. Duddy bitterly resented the thought that he might be the butt of staff-room jokes because of the incident.

Duddy made his way to Eddy's Cigar & Soda, where he found his father drinking coffee with some of the other men. Max Kravitz greeted his son affably by telling the others that Duddy was "a dope like me," unlike Lennie, who had won scholarships all through school. Max, known as Max the Hack because of a journalist's column about him, was said to be on first-name terms with the fabulous Boy Wonder, Jerry Dingleman, the former resident of St. Urbain Street who had acquired great wealth. Max's favourite story, which he repeated now, was of how the Boy Wonder, being absolutely penniless, had begun selling streetcar transfer tickets for three cents each and eventually, having moved to Baltimore, had returned in great luxury. As Max told the story, the men always moved closer, "their fears and hopes riding with the Boy Wonder in Baltimore."

Duddy told his father about Mr. MacPherson, but Max dismissed Duddy as being a troublemaker. Max was about to drive Duddy home when two incidents intervened. MacDonald, one of the men present, offered to show Duddy some dirty pictures, but was rebuked by Max. Then the phone rang. It was a call requiring the services of Josette, the whore who was a friend of the taxidrivers. Duddy laughed proudly when he discovered that his father was a pimp for Josette, and Max gave his son a stinging slap. Duddy had to find his own way home.

Commentary

(1) We discover that Duddy comes by his apparent amorality naturally. For example, his father admires the Boy Wonder greatly, though he is aware of his association with gangsters. Also, though Max objects to Duddy's looking at MacDonald's pictures, he himself is a pimp for Josette.

(2) This chapter enables us to understand Duddy a little more. He is motherless, and his father is obviously not greatly concerned over the boy's welfare. Indeed, without apparently deliberately seeking to hurt Duddy, Max compares Duddy unfavourably with Lennie. In these circumstances, Duddy's ebullience and aggressiveness come as no surprise.

(3) More of the social milieu of the novel is sketched in. The life of the people seems to be strangely rootless: at the beginning of the chapter, Duddy makes his own supper, having arrived home very late; Max is a pimp; and the men in the bar seem to live on the dream of what the Boy Wonder accomplished.

(4) Seemingly apart from this world is Duddy's brother, Lennie. He is the promising student, not heeding Duddy's chatter about the

day's events, financed by his uncle in order to become a professional man, a doctor. He is apart from the social world around him, and yet in a sense he is the embodiment of its dreams. His intelligence will be his means of escape.

Chapter Four

Summary

Next morning, in the school staff-room, there was an energetic discussion. Mr. Coldwell and Mr. Jackson had both received obscene phone calls the previous night and were sure that Duddy Kravitz was responsible. Mr. Coldwell insisted that MacPherson should strap the boy, but he refused to consider strapping Duddy. Mr. Cox approved of MacPherson's stand, but the older teacher offered Cox no encouragement.

On his desk, Mr. MacPherson found a note accusing him of being a coward for refusing to strap. He merely threw it in the waste-paper basket.

Arriving home, MacPherson found a note from Jenny, explaining that she was asleep because Dr. Hanson had given her an injection. Phoning the doctor, MacPherson learned that he was to miss school next morning in order to see the doctor at nine o'clock.

Mrs. Clara Shields phoned, and insisted that he come to a party in their hotel suite. Unable to find a way to refuse the invitation, MacPherson attended the party. He was horrified after "a long time and lots of whiskies" to find that it was three o'clock in the morning. As he travelled home by taxi, he reflected on his evening. It was obvious that they still thought him to be "the freshly scrubbed idealist who had left McGill twenty years ago"; they did not know that he was "exhausted, bitter, and drained." However, he still took comfort from the fact that he had not yet strapped a boy.

At home, he found Jenny crumpled up on the hall floor, the telephone receiver dangling from the hook above her. He telephoned for an ambulance.

Commentary

The chapter is totally devoted to MacPherson and contains three major points of significance. First, MacPherson's pathetic clinging to the principle of not using the strap is emphasized. We already know that the idea behind not strapping is dead; now the unwillingness to strap seems to be identified even more with MacPherson's survival. Second, the teacher's deterioration as a person is underlined once more. Though his wife is obviously seriously ill, he is unable to refuse the invitation to the hotel party. Moreover, once at the party he stays absurdly late. He is thus scarcely a responsible, functioning human being. Finally, this part of the plot is evidently moving towards a crisis. Mrs. MacPherson is near death, and she seems to have collapsed while answering the telephone. The link between this call and Duddy's method of punishing teachers is clear.

Chapter Five

Summary

The boys waited in the classroom for MacPherson, who had been away from school since his wife's death. Cohen declared that his brother had met MacPherson, very drunk, in the Pines and had offered the teacher a drink. When the teacher had slapped Cohen's brother, he had hit him on the jaw.

MacPherson entered in the midst of the uproar. The boys soon discovered that he was drunk. When Kravitz asked a question about the Spanish Inquisition, MacPherson responded with what the boys regarded as an anti-Jewish statement. The boys called MacPherson a Nazi fascist.

Commentary

The part of the plot involving MacPherson has entered a new stage with the death of his wife. The teacher can no longer even appear to cope, as we see from his drunken condition and from his unwise slur upon his Jewish students.

The slur, in itself, is interesting. It is certainly an unfortunate comment to be made by the teacher. However, it is not really so obviously offensive as the boys assume. Their reaction, then, reveals the sensitivity of the Jewish community, which suffers small signs of discrimination continually and is therefore ready to respond, and perhaps respond too readily, to minor irritation.

Chapter Six

Summary

Mr. Coldwell was best at strapping, usually strapping a boy until he cried. Mr. Feeney was next best. However, Mr. MacPherson did not even know how to hold the strap, so that when he strapped Duddy that afternoon the blows were feeble. He strapped fifteen boys that week, with little effect: "the rowdiness in class, and his own drinking, increased in proportion to the strappings."

One night at home, two weeks later, Mr. MacPherson began a new bottle of whisky and thought over his troubles. He sat trying to feel "more than a sense of liberation because Jenny, whom he had once loved truly, was dead." He decided that Duddy Kravitz was the source of all his troubles. He staggered to the telephone and called Duddy's number. A voice unknown to him answered. He slammed down the receiver after identifying himself and stumbled back to the living room. The first thing he noticed were the history test papers, which he flung into the fireplace. Exhausted, he watched them burn.

Chapter Seven

Summary

Mr. Leonard Bush, the principal of Fletcher's Field High School, was besieged by complaints. The latest was that of Max Kravitz, who objected to Mr. MacPherson's calling the boys dirty Jews and to Mr. MacPherson's phoning at three o'clock in the morning. Mr. Bush tried to make excuses, but he knew that something would have to be done about MacPherson. His drinking, for example, had become a school joke. Consequently, next morning he invited Mac-Pherson to have a chat with him after school.

That day, Mr. MacPherson found himself confronted by the boys over the problem of the unreturned history tests. They were led by Duddy, who put out his cigarette before addressing the teacher. At a loss, Mr. MacPherson plunged into the task of calling the register, which he had not checked all week. His troubles had come home sharply to him: his drinking, the phone call, Duddy's dominance in the classroom, his ostracization in the staff room. Thus when he came to the name Kravitz, he walked towards the boy and accused him of killing his wife. Duddy defied the teacher, who passed out before further trouble developed. Duddy refused to accept MacPherson's accusation, claiming that he did not mean any harm in making the phone call.

Mr. Bush suggested that Mr. MacPherson should stay home for a few days. As the teacher left the school, he encountered Duddy outside. Smiling a little, his words to the boy were startling: "You'll go far, Kravitz. You're going to go very far."

The rest of this chapter gives a comic account of the march of the Fletcher's cadets.

Commentary

(1) This chapter marks the disappearance of Mr. MacPherson from the narrative. His "demise" has been effectively accomplished by Duddy. Of course, the teacher's decline had begun long before he met Duddy, but Kravitz's intransigence and his act of phoning the MacPhersons in the middle of the night had directly caused two critical events in the teacher's life — the death of Mrs. MacPherson and the first strappings administered in twenty years. MacPherson was not resilient enough to withstand either of these. That Mr. MacPherson's end was inevitable is fairly obvious. However, that Duddy's behaviour and actions were monstrous is equally obvious. It is clear, then, that Duddy is not to be a conventional hero, offering the reader laudable actions and admirable values.

(2) The importance of MacPherson's words to Duddy – "You'll go far, Kravitz. You're going to go very far" – must not be under-estimated. They may simply be a recognition by MacPherson that Duddy possesses the kind of resilience, not to say absolute hardness, which MacPherson himself has lacked, with the result that a career which began with idealism petered out into feelings of futility and disillusionment. On the other hand, the words may involve a larger recognition. It may be that MacPherson has seen in Duddy's unflinching amorality the kind of value that the world cherised. Perhaps, in MacPherson's eyes Duddy possessed the quality that the world rewarded. If that is indeed so, then the teacher's words have the quality of prophecy for Duddy.

(3) The account of the march of the Fletcher's cadets is surely not intended for simple comic relief. Its juxtaposition in the narra-tive with the end of the MacPherson story is interesting, and perhaps serves to emphasize the gulf between the world of MacPherson and the world of Kravitz. The incident of the march reveals the people of Duddy's world with the kind of irreverential earthiness and spon-taneous humanity that could only be incomprehensible to a man like MacPherson.

Chapter Eight

Summary

Simcha Kravitz, Duddy's grandfather, had come to Montreal from Poland forty-eight years earlier. He was a shoemaker, and eventually had his own shop, above which he and his family lived.

He was respected by others for his honesty and wisdom, but he was not loved because of his silent strength of character. Some idolized him; others resented him. However, his stature increased when it became known that even the gentiles of the district respected him. That respect was won when he set the broken leg of a French Canadian, Blondin, before the arrival of the doctor.

Though Simcha would not talk about his private life, his love for his first-born son, Benjy, was obvious. Those who respected Simcha hoped that Benjy would compensate for the old man's unhappy life with his wife; those who resented Simcha hoped that Benjy would have bad luck. However, Benjy prospered, and by the age of twenty-six was the owner of a basement blouse factory. Moreover, he paid the highest wages and, like his father, lent money and never repeated a confidence. Even when Benjy began to read the works of radical authors and ceased attending the synagogue, Simcha did not reprove his son.

When Benjy married Ida, the daughter of a pants presser, Simcha took his daughter-in-law to his heart, for the marriage seemed to be a happy one. Then trouble began after the death of Simcha's wife. Ida began taking trips, and Benjy did not visit his father often. The old man began to pay more attention to Duddy, the son of Max.

After a mysterious visit from which Benjy departed with what looked like a jar of preserves, Simcha declared that both he and his son Benjy were failures in this new land, for, he stated, "a man without land is nobody."

Duddy was seven at the time and a year earlier his mother had enrolled him in the parochial school, for which Uncle Benjy paid. At this time, the old man frequently walked hand in hand with his grandson, a scene reminiscent of his walks with his son in days gone by. Now, however, Simcha did not have enemies. The old men decided that Duddy was a mean, crafty boy and only hoped that he would not hurt Simcha too much.

Commentary

(1)   This chapter establishes what might be described as the polarity within Duddy's character. On the one hand, from an early age he

has been influenced by his grandfather, a man of integrity and piety, so that the boy was enrolled in the Jewish parochial school. On the other hand, we are confronted by the judgement of the old men, who declare Duddy to be a mean and crafty boy.

(2)   Of great importance in the narrative are the words of the grandfather to Duddy: "A man without land is nobody. Remember that, Duddel." These words are to provide a focus for Duddy's acquisitive energies and lead directly to the powerful final scene of the novel. Indeed, the words become a kind of motif linking episodes in the novel, a kind of refrain which is never far from Duddy's thoughts.

Chapter Nine

Summary

Until he was thirteen years old, Duddy was at the parochial school, where he met many boys who were better off than he was. He fought those who were not too big for him to fight with; the others he befriended and taught dubious habits, such as stealing and cheating. After three years the mothers warned their children not to play with Duddy, but nevertheless those who were excluded from his gang, the Warriors, felt the snub deeply.

One of the rejected was Milty Halpirin, the spoiled child of a real-estate agent, who yearned to be a Warrior. Duddy finally agreed to initiate him into the gang if he would first drink a nauseating potion. No sooner had Milty drunk the concoction than Duddy pretended hysteria and declared that a terrible mistake had been made; now Milty's penis would fall off, and his pubic hair would never grow. Milty became violently ill, and Duddy became the first boy ever to be expelled for a week. Duddy had his revenge a week later when he and three Warriors visited the house of the Halpirins. With the unwitting assistance of Milty, they destroyed all of the tulips of Mrs. Halpirin, who was an amateur horticulturist.

Since it was wartime, a kind of civil defence organization, the Canadian Provost Corps, had sprung up in Montreal. The St. Urbain Street detachment was led by Benny Feinberg, a middle-aged man who was the butt of many jokes because of his inordinate pride in his uniform. At first, the Warriors were the allies of the CPC. Feinberg assured them that Montreal might well be devastated. Therefore, for example, they even contemplated painting a bullseye on the roof of the synagogue. But when Duddy learned that Feinberg had given a real first-aid kit to the YMHA, the Warriors decided to have their revenge upon the CPC. The opportunity came during a practice blackout. As Feinberg and his men checked for windows showing any light, St. Urbain Street suddenly became a blaze of light. Duddy and his friends had sprinkled the whole street with kerosene, which they ignited at the propitious moment. Afterwards, some said that the communists were responsible for the happening; others blamed the fascists; the newspaper declared it to be the work of juvenile delinquents. However, Feinberg stopped wearing his uniform.

Commentary

The first seven chapters were largely devoted to the MacPherson sub-plot, giving a kind of picture of Duddy as he is through most of the book. Chapters eight and nine begin the process of looking back into Duddy's childhood. Chapter nine establishes the fact that Duddy's personality and behaviour were well indicated from an early age: the amorality, the fascination he held for others, the ruthlessness and the ingenuity are all evident in his younger years.

Chapter Ten

Summary

Duddy engaged in a variety of commercial activities while at parochial school. He made money by defrauding stamp companies who sent stamps on approval to minors, and he rented out twenty-cent American comic books at three cents a day. His venture into selling pornographic comic books ended in financial disaster when his supplier was arrested by the police. In addition, he made money by selling hockey sticks which he had stolen from the Montreal Forum.

Duddy took his first regular job in 1945, at the age of thirteen. He worked for the summer in his Uncle Benjy's dress factory. The work was boring, but it brought Duddy into association with twelve French-Canadian girls, who sewed belts. At first, he did not understand the talk and giggles of the girls, but when at last he did he followed one of them out of the workroom. Unfortunately for Duddy, Benjy passed by a half hour later and, seeing that Duddy and Adele were gone, guessed where they were. Duddy was transferred to the cutting room.

Uncle Benjy was a wealthy but disappointed man. His marriage had brought no children, and Ida went to Florida every winter, where she met other men. But he loved his wife, and in his more drunken moments would clasp her fiercely to him as he slept. When his father finally asked why there were no children, Benjy confessed that he was impotent. The old man gave Benjy an old country remedy which he flushed down the toilet. Father and son did not discuss the matter again.

The socialist magazines to which he subscribed bored Benjy with their mixture of foolishness and romance, but he became known as a supporter of communist causes. He refused to contribute to the synagogue building fund, and taunted fellow manufacturers with his communist sympathies. Thus he made more money and more enemies. Yet he got along no better with the communists who came to see him. In spite of all of his prodigious reading, he could not find any answer to the question which tormented: why he, a fat factory owner, was "hopelessly in love with a woman who dyed her hair, wore too much rouge, and preferred contract bridge to Bach." Meanwhile, he helped to keep the family together and drank alone.

Thus, when Max got married, Benjy set his brother up with a taxi cab. And he would do anything for Lennie, treating the boy as his own son. But Benjy felt differently about Duddy. The boy's apparent craftiness, his restlessness and poor physical appearance made a bad impression on the uncle. However, Benjy was prepared to give the boy a chance. Unfortunately, two weeks after being transferred to the cutting room, Duddy reported to his uncle that a worker was stealing cloth. Benjy was displeased; he did not, he declared, employ anyone to spy on the workers. Moreover, he did not like Duddy's practice of selling mail-order underwear and other articles to the girls. But he would not fire Duddy, for that would hurt Simcha. Nevertheless, Duddy felt that he had been humiliated, and he never worked for Benjy again. The boy began to identify more and more with the Boy Wonder, who was not an atheist like Uncle Benjy. Duddy wanted to be somebody, and he continued to put money in the bank. He had never forgotten his grandfather's words: "A man without land is nobody."

At Fletcher's Field High School, the crowd assembled, "too soon and thirsty and proud," to witness the graduation of the class of '49. The ritual, complete with Mr. Bush's abstract urgings, a Chopin piano solo and an irrelevant speech by a United Empire Loyalist, did not suppress the irreverent earthiness of the assembled parents, whose attention was concentrated on their own sons and daughters. Duddy was the four-hundred-and-tenth boy to be handed his diploma.

He had graduated third class with failures in history and algebra. He turned sharply away from Mr. MacPherson's emtpy chair as he left the platform.

Commentary

(1)   Duddy's fierce dedication to his grandfather's words is emphasized. Resentful of what he considers to be Uncle Benjy's humiliating treatment, he adopts as his model the Boy Wonder, whose material success inspires Duddy to emulation. That he may achieve his goal is shown to be a strong possibility. Already, the boy has been for some time a resourceful entrepreneur: he has made money with the stolen stamps and hockey sticks; he has worked for Uncle Benjy; and he has sold items to the factory girls. Thus he has displayed a restless acquisitiveness unfettered by ethical considerations. His dedication to his purpose is, of course, understandable. He is not really liked. He cannot emulate the scholastic success of his brother, a fact which seems to embarrass his grandfather; he is not, obviously, popular with his teachers; and his own uncle dislikes him. Duddy thus undoubtedly feels compelled to prove his worth in the only way he understands.

(2)   We notice again the strange disjunction between the Jewish world of St. Urbain Street and the world which surrounds it. The ritual of the commencement is an Anglo-Saxon ritual: the teachers are Anglo-Saxon, and the guest speaker is Anglo-Saxon. That Anglo-Saxon world stresses abstractions; the Jewish world seems to concern itself with more mundane, everyday matters. It is scarcely surprising that such an environment spawned Duddy Kravitz. Coming from a people whose Jewishness was not always appreciated and from a family in which he lacked both love and money, Duddy might well be expected to use his birthright — his wits.

Chapter Eleven

Summary

Duddy found the land he wanted by accident, for that same summer he obtained work as a waiter at Ste Agathe des Monts, in the Laurentian mountains. The other waiters were college boys and had not attended Fletcher's Field High School, since they were more prosperous than Duddy. Thus he was not accepted by them. His situation was not improved when, because of his quickness, he was given three extra tables.

One of Duddy's enemies was Irwin Shubert, son of a prominent criminal lawyer, for whom a bright future was foretold. Duddy had alienated Irwin on the second day by recommending some sexy literature, while Irwin pretended only professional interest in the medical volume that was his prize possession. Moreover, Duddy laughed at Irwin's stories about having a gift of hypnotism and about women and whips and boy-scout masters. Consequently, Irwin constantly baited Duddy. In addition, Irwin led the other boys to believe that Duddy was stealing money from their wallets. The trouble between the two boys came to a head when Duddy discovered Irwin masturbating at three o'clock in the morning. In revenge, Irwin informed Linda Rubin, the daughter of the owner, that Duddy had stolen money from the boys.

Duddy was even more shunned by the college boy waiters after the episode with the whisky. He found the bottle, apparently a gift from a departing guest, on his cot. Though he thought of sending the liquor to his grandfather as a gift, Duddy was persuaded by Irwin to share it with the other boys. The bottle apparently contained urine, and, confused, no one would seem to believe Duddy's protestations that he had found the bottle on the bed.

Being thus shut out by his colleagues, Duddy began to explore Ste Agathe on his free time.

About sixty miles from Montreal, Ste Agathe des Monts had become the resort of the Jewish middle class. Here, as they prospered they bought land and built cottages, boat houses and hotels.

Although Rubin's was only one of many Jewish hotels, it was distinguished by having the undisputed number-one comic of Ste Agathe, Cuckoo Kaplan, who had played nightclubs in the United States. Short and frantic, he entertained the guests with madcap actions, such as breaking an egg over the head of a bald man. Duddy, too, was impressed with Cuckoo and used to visit the comedian often in his room, where he would sometimes try out new routines on Duddy. The two also exchanged confidences, Kaplan claiming that one day he would be very famous, and Duddy explaining his plans to make money by showing movies at all of the resorts and by making films of weddings and bar mitzvahs. Duddy even declared that one day he would make a feature-length film starring Cuckoo.

Cuckoo also hated Irwin Shubert, for one night, being stuck with a large bar bill, Irwin and a friend had phoned Cuckoo to ask him to come to meet a Broadway producer who was looking for talent. Not until he had paid the large bar bill for two and waited over two hours did Cuckoo realize that he had been the victim of a practical joke. The comedian's only revenge was to mimic Irwin comically at the beach, but Duddy warned him against the practice, because rumour had it that Irwin and Rubin's daughter were going to get married.

Duddy also told Cuckoo about an idea for a Laurentian newspaper, which would be sent to Americans who had stayed in Ste Agathe. He thought that the advertising potential was great, and intended to speak to the Boy Wonder about it in the fall.

However, though Duddy had been putting money in the bank since he was eleven, and though in his first month at Rubin's he had made nearly three hundred dollars in tips, he was acutely conscious of how little money he had in terms of business. He wanted to be somebody, but despaired when he thought of all the good ideas from which people had already made money. He felt that time was short, since he was already seventeen and a half. He needed money, and decided to see the Boy Wonder after summer. Meanwhile, he scrutinized carefully the behaviour of the business men upon whom he waited.

All the while he dreamed, Irwin tormented him, in spite of the protestations of the other boys. Duddy retaliated by singing bawdy songs about masturbation.

Commentary

Prominent in this chapter is Duddy's sense of isolation. Even among his contemporaries, he is regarded as inferior because of his lack of money and educaton. This feeling is one of the reasons for his friendship with Cuckoo, whose ambitions are obviously too great for his talent. This feeling is also the reason for Duddy's dedication to his dreams of making money, dreams which are not without an admirable ingenuity.

Chapter Twelve

Summary

With the coming of July, the hottest and most gruelling month of the season, the young waiters felt drained of energy. They quarrelled more and rested more. Duddy was the only one who did not stop, so that he could earn extra tips. For that reason, Irwin decided to teach him a lesson.

One day, Duddy entered the dormitory to shave and shine his shoes. He had a date with Linda. He was both pleased and nervous at the same time. His experience with girls was limited. He could only rely on the whispered comments of the boys and the behaviour of the men at the hotel who spent the summer trying to seduce girls. He had refused to pay attention to Yvette, though Cuckoo had told him that she had a real "lust" for Duddy. But Linda was different. She was attractive, "nifty enough for one of those snazzy fashion magazines," assured, and nineteen years of age. Duddy could not understand why she had suggested that he take her out. On their date, he could not see that Linda was really making fun of him. At one point, she left him for an hour, departing in the company of a painter, Peter Butler, and returning an hour later, her face flushed and bits of dead leaves stuck to her dress. However, as he drank more Duddy felt that Linda was really interested in him. He talked of what he wanted for the future, and he told some lies about himself and the Boy Wonder. Not really understanding what was happening, Duddy found himself in a befuddled state at the end of the evening, having agreed to act as banker for a roulette game in the recreation hall at one a.m. Monday morning.

Commentary

This chapter depicts clearly Duddy's vulnerability. Naive and gauche, he is the object of ridicule for those around him who are wealthier and more sophisticated. However, such is his desire to succeed that he is ready to believe that a rich, spoiled girl like Linda can really be interested in him. He is completely unaware of how foolish he appears with his tasteless dress and grandiose stories. The joke which Linda and Irwin are to play upon him is to strike at him where he is most vulnerable — his money, or rather his passionate desire for it.

Chapter Thirteen

Summary

In the three days before the roulette game, Duddy was nervous, fearing for his money. However, the guests, knowing he was to be the banker, began to pay more attention to him, and Duddy enjoyed the experience. Thus he put on an outward show of bravado. However, in case of disaster he withdrew three hundred dollars from his bank account.

For a while, things went well for Duddy in the game. But when he allowed the players to raise the stakes, Irwin began to bet in earnest and was soon winning heavily. Others began to bet with Irwin, and Duddy's hands started to shake as his money disappeared. Cuckoo challenged Irwin, declaring that he knew it was Irwin's roulette wheel, but Irwin was relentless. Soon Duddy was broke. The hotel guests, embarrassed, filed out; Irwin was jubilant.

Duddy rushed out to be alone on the beach. He was hurt at losing all of his money and hurt at the thought of being a laughingstock. Rubin, Cuckoo, Linda and others began to be anxious at his absence and set out to search for him. As he listened to their cries in the darkness, Duddy began to laugh at them. He deliberately evaded them, running through the woods and approaching Ste Agathe from another direction.

At a French-Canadian chip place he met Yvette, to whom he told the events of the night. Together they went for a walk and made love. They arranged to go swimming on Wednesday afternoon.

When Duddy returned to the hotel at nine o'clock, he was greeted effusively by the guests and no less effusively by an anxious Mr. Rubin, who promptly gave him two days off. In the dormitory, Duddy was approached by Irwin, who, forced by two colleagues, returned Duddy's three hundred dollars. That night, the guests made a collection for Duddy and presented him with an envelope containing almost five hundred dollars. Duddy was jubilant, so that when Linda came to apologize he was aggressively rude. He declared that he knew what she really thought of him, but asserted that one day he would be somebody. Moreover, he confessed defiantly that his father was a taxicab driver and a pimp.

The next morning he gave Rubin his notice, but agreed to stay on for another week if he was given a room to himself. Rubin hoped that Duddy, his quickest boy, would stay on for the season.

Commentary

Like the hero in a picaresque novel, Duddy has emerged from his misfortune rather well. In fact, he has made a handsome financial profit. However, two things are worthy of note. In the first place, this experience has made Duddy acutely aware of what others think about him. As a result, he becomes even more determined to pursue his goals. Further, his words to the repentant Irwin are interesting: "Cheaters never prosper. I hope this'll be a good lesson to you. I hope you profit from it in the future." To anyone aware of the future career of Duddy, the words have powerful ironic effect. If anything, at this point they are strongly reminiscent of the moral platitudes of his father, Max, who is hardly a character of great moral strength.

Chapter Fourteen

Summary

On Wednesday afternoon, Duddy met Yvette, who insisted on taking him "somewhere special. Another lake." He wondered if she realized that he was embarrassed to be seen with her.

After a long walk over the mountain and through some fields and woods, she showed him the lake. Duddy was ecstatic. He ran naked into the water, swimming and diving excitedly. He had found his land. Feverishly, he made Yvette promise never to tell anyone else about the lake and insulted her by offering her fifty dollars to keep her promise. He talked excitedly about his plans for buying and building, explaining that he would need her help, since farmers might be wary of selling to someone who was not French Canadian. He did not have more than two thousand dollars saved, and he would need her help to act for him. He was too young to marry, he explained, and if he did marry he might of necessity have to marry a rich woman. But he would give Yvette a share of the profits if she helped him, and he would leave her money, before departing for Montreal, to take care of initial expenses.

In spite of the late hour, Duddy could not help sharing the news of his find with Cuckoo on returning to the hotel. The boy was in such a state of excitement that he fainted and had to be carried to his room.

Next morning he left early. Linda declared that the reason for his sudden leave-taking must be that he had got Yvette pregnant. She laughed at the thought of Duddy's boasts about being an intimate of Jerry Dingleman, for she was always invited to the Boy Wonder's parties when she was in Montreal. Cuckoo made the mistake of mentioning Duddy's find to Linda.

Commentary

Part one of the novel ends with Duddy on the threshold of manhood. His dreams now have an objective reality upon which to focus; he has found the land he wants. He is now obviously to embark upon a testing period in which his strength of purpose is to be tried. Whatever the material future which awaits him, it is surely ominous to observe the effect which the "find" has upon Duddy as a person. This is seen clearly in his relationship with Yvette. Duddy has been surprised at the girl's interest in him, and with her he has experienced sexual intercourse for the first time. However, Duddy shows no tenderness or appreciation for Yvette. He is embarrassed to be seen with her. In his almost hysterical joy on seeing the lake, he abuses her feelings, insisting roughly that she should not tell anyone about the lake and talking callously of his inability to marry. Duddy may well have suffered from not knowing love and tenderness from others in his life, but in this scene he surely demonstrates an incapacity for bestowing love and tenderness upon others.

Part Two

Chapter One

Summary

On returning to Montreal, Duddy sought out his father at Eddy's Cigar & Soda. Max was somewhat embarrassed by Duddy's show of affection and drove his son home.

Duddy learned that Lennie was still studying hard and was to be sent by Uncle Benjy for a two-week holiday. After giving his brother thirty dollars, Duddy also learned that Lennie had a new girl friend, a gentile, and that he had a new set of friends, mostly non-Jewish and from good families.

After Lennie and Max had left, Duddy began to cry, perhaps because he was feeling feverish, perhaps because he was home again.

Simcha was delighted to see Duddy again, taking pleasure in the boy's increasing maturity. However, he accepted the news of the land cynically and accepted Duddy's gift of things for the farm without comment.

At home, Duddy waited up for his father, who did not appear until almost two o'clock. Duddy wanted Max to make an appointment to see the Boy Wonder. Max was both derisive and evasive; he declared that in any case the Boy Wonder was away in Florida for two weeks. Their discussion, which became quite heated, was interrupted by the doorbell. Lennie was standing outside, drunk. Duddy avoided Max's seeing Lennie, who claimed that he was never going to be a doctor because he had ruined his life. Duddy got him settled in bed without Max's being aware of the disturbance.

Two weeks later, after much reluctance again, Max promised to make an appointment for Duddy to see the Boy Wonder.

Commentary

(1) Duddy's position in his family is emphasized, as we witness Max rejecting his son's show of affection at the begnning of the chapter, thinking again only of Lennie.

(2) Max's shallowness and empty pride are underlined. He talks in cliches – "When I lose my temper I lose my temper" – and his close relationship with the Boy Wonder is obviously largely mythical.

(3) The plot is approaching another step in development, as Duddy prepares to approach the Boy Wonder, who is the next necessary stage in the accomplishment of his dreams.

Chapter Two

Summary

While waiting to be introduced to the Boy Wonder, Duddy estimated that he would need at least fifteen thousand dollars down for the land. He did not remain idle: he drove his father's cab at night; during the day, he sold liquid soap and toilet supplies to factories, for which he had bought a cheap used car. He also attended a business administration course at Wellington College.

At the Wellington College ciné club he met Peter John Friar, a bearded Englishman who was introduced as a distinguished director of documentary films but who, Duddy judged, was "something of a lush." After consuming many drinks, Friar arranged for Duddy to come to his flat the next day to discuss the boy's idea for making films of weddings and bar mitzvahs. They came to an arrangement quickly. Friar would be given five hundred dollars for equipment and would receive one-third of the profits. Duddy opened an office under the name of Dudley Kane Enterprises.

Duddy needed money urgently: the office cost one hundred dollars a month; he had to give up driving the cab in case he met any potential customers for the movie business; he had no clients yet for the films; and Yvette had sent him detailed maps and information about the land in Ste Agathe showing him that for all the land he needed twenty thousand dollars in cash and mortgages to the extent of thirty thousand. Further, a crisis came when Yvette told him that one of the owners wanted to sell at once. She had put down a deposit of two hundred and fifty dollars towards the total down payment of thirty-two hundred dollars. Duddy had only six hundred dollars in the bank.

Consequently, Duddy hurried to find clients for whom he could make films. The first, Mr. Cohen, proved difficult, but finally agreed to let Duddy make a film of his boy's bar mitzvah, after reducing the price from two thousand dollars to twelve hundred dollars. Mr. Seigal became a second client, paying a two-hundred-and-fifty dollar deposit, for a total of fifteen hundred if he liked the film, and only eight hundred and fifty if he did not. He could not get other clients; some were interested but wanted to see a finished film first.

Commentary

The key note of the chapter is its building tension. Urged on by his dreams, Duddy now has to come to grips with reality. The dreamland has now become something to be paid for. Grappling with that fact, Duddy has to trust in the uncertain idea of making films, an idea made all the more uncertain by his alliance with the "arty" Mr. Friar.

Chapter Three

Summary

Duddy awoke screaming at three a.m., having a nightmare about his land. Afterwards, Max, Lennie and Duddy remained awake, talking. As Max began to talk about his dead wife, Duddy wanted to ask his father whether she had loved Duddy, but Max was not interested in talking further.

Almost as an afterthought, Max mentioned that the Boy Wonder would see Duddy the next day.

Commentary

(1) There is an indication again of Duddy's desperate desire to be loved. He has been aware previously that if he had been Lennie, Uncle Benjy would have lent him the money he needed so desperately. Now, his desire for affection focuses on his dead mother.

(2)   The plot is advanced a stage further with the meeting between Duddy and the Boy Wonder. Dream is again to become reality.

Chapter Four

Summary

Jerry Dingleman, the Boy Wonder, had once been a handsome man, engaged to Olive Brucker, whose father was wealthy. But at the age of twenty-eight he had been struck by polio. Mr. Brucker had immediately sent his daughter to Europe. Eventually she had gone through three husbands, had psychiatric problems and was rumoured to be seeing Dingleman occasionally. Now, at thirty, Dingleman, walking with the help of crutches, was no longer handsome, and strange stories were circulated about his sex life.

Every Wednesday, Dingleman received a stream of suppliants asking for favours. When Duddy arrived, he was not even allowed to see the Boy Wonder. Shub, Dingleman's punch-drunk assistant, passed on the message that Duddy was offered a job as a busboy at one of Dingleman's establishments. Even when Duddy barged into Dingleman's office, the Boy Wonder was derisive about Duddy's plans. Duddy ran out after shouting an obscenity. Dingleman seemed to be interested in the boy's reaction and ordered his car so that he could follow the boy.

Commentary

Reality has proven to be discomforting for Duddy. First, he has obviously seen clearly Max's real relationship to the Boy Wonder; his father has little influence. Secondly, the Boy Wonder, the myth of St. Urbain Street, is hardly the ideal figure of legend. He is presented here as a busy, unfeeling manipulator of people.

Chapter Five

Summary

At Eddy's, Duddy berated his father for the false stories about the Boy Wonder. However, Dingleman appeared. He wanted Duddy to go to New York with him that night. They would be gone two or three days and would have a chance to discuss Duddy's business proposition. Later, Dingleman assured Shub that Duddy was perfect to take on the trip because he was so innocent.

In New York, Duddy had difficulty in speaking to Dingleman, who did not regard the boy's plans seriously. The Boy Wonder seemed to be busy constantly with his own business, part of the time being spent getting rid of a woman who appeared to be asking for more drugs. However, Duddy did arrange to buy some pinball machines, which had been outlawed in New York and which were to be transported across the border for him.

At the station, Dingleman gave Duddy a suitcase to carry back to Canada and explained that they were going to travel separately. He also lent Duddy five hundred dollars. Duddy was worried by the strange behaviour, but the suitcase seemed harmless. One of the items it contained was a coffee can with unfamiliar powder inside; Duddy did not recognize it as heroin. However, he crossed the border safely and handed over the suitcase to Shub.

Commentary

This chapter brings some of the characters into sharper focus. At the beginning, Max's fawning upon the Boy Wonder underlines the cab driver's lack of consequence; he means nothing to Dingleman. The Boy Wonder's callous indifference is stressed. Duddy's plans mean nothing to him; they are a source of amusement. Dingleman's connection with drug-trafficking and his callous exploitation of Duddy's naiveté portray clearly the heartless nature of the man. More and more we see Duddy obsessed with his desire to launch into his enterprises in order that he might buy land. His desire is not calculated; it is feverish.

Chapter Six

Summary

The Cohen boy's bar mitzvah took place at a fashionable temple run by a very fashionable rabbi, Harvey Goldstone, for an equally fashionable congregation. Uncle Benjy condemned the temple as a "religious drugstore," and even Jerry Dingleman said that when he stepped inside he felt like "a Jesuit in a whorehouse."

After the film had been shot, Duddy began to be nervous. Mr. Friar was depressed because his best roll of film had been overexposed. However, after the editing Friar was exultant. The film, he declared, should be entered in the Cannes Festival; it was his best work to date. When he saw the film, Duddy took to his bed for two days. He thought that Mr. Cohen would refuse it. It was not a film of a family event; it was arty and symbolic. However, he saw Mr. Cohen and stated that the film was not for sale, that it was to be entered at Cannes. Mr. Cohen's family became intrigued. They obliged Cohen to pay twenty-five hundred dollars to become a silent partner in having the film distributed commercially. They were even more enthusiastic when they saw the film, with its florid sound commentary and family shots.

With his cheque, Duddy instructed Yvette to pay Brault for his land and to put the balance in her account.

Commentary

The chapter is largely satirical in nature. There is a devastatingly comic description of the reformed Jewish temple, complete with a rabbi more interested in his image than in his work. The satire extends to the successful Jewish family, revelling in the social status of having a family event filmed. Finally, the hilarious screenplay for the film is a biting exposé of the florid, overstated art film.

Chapter Seven

Summary

When Duddy came home, Lennie had left a note saying that he was leaving and would not be going to medical school. Both Max and Benjy were distraught, but Duddy persuaded them to get some sleep by assuring them that he would begin looking for Lennie the next day.

After the next bar mitzvah film, Duddy was a great success. He told Yvette that he now had enough contracts to carry them through to next January, with a gross of eight to ten thousand dollars. He was also going to make a film next summer at Grossman's Camp Forest Land, chiefly in order to get inside information on how to run a camp. Duddy, Yvette and Friar went out to celebrate, but Duddy's gaucheness and unfettered good spirits annoyed his companions. He declared that he was now going to get an apartment of his own.

Duddy was perturbed that he had to go looking for Lennie, just when his business needed him. However, he admired his brother and was determined to find him. Lennie and he had once been close, though since Lennie had entered medical school things had changed.

Commentary

Duddy's treatment of Yvette is significant. She has not only been his lover; she is also a valuable ally in his land dealing. However, even Friar can see that Duddy will not marry Yvette, who is treated casually by Duddy. Their night of celebration portrays clearly Duddy's unawareness of the feelings of others.

On the other hand, Duddy's attachment to his brother is strong. Lennie has been spoiled by Benjy, and yet Duddy holds no grudge against his brother. Duddy regards him with undiminished admiration and concern.

Chapter Eight

Summary

Duddy went to see Riva, who had been Lennie's girlfriend, but she had not seen Lennie for some time. Then Bernie, whom Duddy met at the Hillel House, passed on the infromation that Lennie had changed. At first he had been studious. Then, associating with the more socially aware Riva, he had come out of his shell. But he had become possessive of Riva and an ugly quarrel had ensued, which had alienated the other students at Hillel House from Lennie. Duddy's brother had then associated with a largely gentile group of wealthy students from Westmount. Irwin Shubert was one of them. Lennie had also been seen with Sandra Calder, daughter of a Westmount millionaire, though Bernie explained, somewhat puzzled, that she was really the girlfriend of Andy Simpson, an Olympic hockey player. Sandra was sick at home at the moment.

Duddy went to the Calders' huge Westmount mansion but was unable to get to see Sandra. He consoled himself by poring over the maps of the Ste Agathe property. That night Bernie took him to a bar where students gathered. The teasing of the students about Lennie being the suicide type did not amuse Duddy.

At home, Duddy told his father what news he had, omitting the part about Lennie's quarrel with Riva and about the students' mention of suicide. Uncle Benjy was fast asleep on the couch, drunk. Ida had been supposed to stay with him two months, but she had left for Florida again after one day. Benjy could not even follow her, because he was refused admission to the States on account of his support of socialist causes.

Commentary

Part of Richler's theme is the desire of the poor Jew for social recognition. That desire is portrayed with pathos in the case of Lennie, an able student who, under pressure, is flattered by the attention paid to him by wealthy gentiles. The gap between the world of St. Urbain Street and the world of Westmount is obviously vast, as we see from Duddy's wonderment at the location and size of the Calder mansion.

Chapter Nine

Summary

After procrastinating by reading the newspaper advertising apartments for rent, Duddy returned to the Calder house. He forced his way in, and Sandra agreed to speak to him. He was to tell Lennie that everything was all right, that Dr. Westcott, even though he was furious, would not say anything. At that point, Duddy admitted that he did not know where Lennie was, and demanded his address. Sandra gave it to him only after Duddy threatened to tell her father what was happening.

Before he left, Duddy could not curb his self-importance. He gave Sandra his business card, declaring that he would reward her if she could get him some film business in Westmount.

Commentary

This chapter is largely a step in the mysterious sub plot involving Lennie. However, Duddy's brash ignorance is apparent once more in his breezy endeavour to persuade Sandra Calder to obtain film busines for him from the gentiles of her social set.

Chapter Ten

Summary

Lennie was in Toronto and Duddy made preparations to go there. He left Friar a hundred dollars for expenses in connection with the movie for the Seigals, and asked him to take Yvette out to dinner.

In Toronto, Duddy found Lennie and learned what had happened. First Lennie had been flattered by the attention of the wealthy gentile set. Encouraged by Irwin, who was also flattered by the group, he had become one of them. Then Irwin informed him that Sandra was pregnant by Andy Simpson. He wanted Lennie to perform an abortion. Lennie had refused. However, he had then been shut out by the group and had at last agreed to perform the operation. During it, Irwin had panicked and phoned Dr. Westcott, who had been furious, though he did not know who was responsible for what had happened. Feeling sure that we would be exposed, Lennie had fled to Toronto, giving up any idea of medical school.

Duddy declared that he was going to inform Mr. Calder of all that had happened. He could see no other way of getting Lennie out of his difficulties. He persuaded his brother to return to Montreal.

On their return, Lennie received an enthusiastic welcome from Max. Duddy had to go straight to his office, where Yvette informed him that more land was on the market, and that Duddy now needed a down payment of twenty-five hundred dollars to obtain it. He phoned Mr. Seigal to ask for an advance of five hundred dollars, but learned that Mr. Friar had just been given that much. Duddy was unconcerned. He insisted that Yvette and he have sexual intercourse immediately. Afterwards, he coarsely remarked that some men must be stupid to get married when there were so many women around. He dismissed Yvette's remark that people do fall in love.

Duddy took his revenge upon Irwin by dictating a letter to the FBI informing them that Shubert was a communist and a sexual pervert. Duddy was seeking to foil Irwin's plans for renting a cottage in Maine that summer.

Commentary

Duddy is emerging more and more as an energetic and practised manipulator. His handling of the Lennie situation is decisive and realistic. He sees the situation objectively and realizes that the only way to set things right for Lennie is to confront Mr. Calder with the truth. He is shrewd enough to know that Lennie cannot find real help from his gentile friends. In addition, Duddy's business is thriving under the care of similar shrewdness and decisiveness. However, he is still strangely blind to his own careless acceptance of Yvette's affections.

Chapter Eleven

Summary

Hugh Thomas Calder had inherited the family fortune but had added to it steadily and without flair. Bored, he was on occasion eccentric.

For example he would sometimes drop a one-hundred-dollar bill
down a urinal and speculate on who would grovel for it. He detested
Dr. Westcott and knew there was something more wrong with Sandra
than a mere nervous upset, but he would not give the doctor the
pleasure of asking. It was bound to be sordid, because his daughter
was "a shallow little bitch." Thus he was not in a receptive mood
when Duddy called.

Duddy immediately revealed the events involving Lennie. Mr.
Calder was intrigued by Duddy's directness and lack of sophistication.
He wanted to know how Duddy got into the film business. Duddy
mentioned his connection with the Boy Wonder, and was astonished
to find that Calder had not heard of Dingleman. Calder finally
promised to see to it that Westcott would not say anything about what
had happened, but he asked Duddy to telephone him so that they
could have dinner together.

Commentary

The chapter is interesting for the confrontation between Duddy, the
hero who can be astonishingly naive on occasion, and Hugh Calder,
the sophisticated and rather bored representative of Montreal's Anglo-
Saxon upper class. On this occasion, it is Duddy's very naiveté which
wins the day for him, though he would be unaware of the reason for
his victory. Exercised in suitable circumstances, that naiveté can be
a refreshing, sincere quality.

Chapter Twelve

Summary

Duddy had problems. Cohen was upset because a commercial producer had dismissed his film as "Amateur night in Dixie," and Friar
was still missing with the five hundred dollars, and the Seigal bar
mitzvah was only two days away. However, he moved into an apartment. Unthinkingly, he complained of the *goy* smell in front of
Yvette, who lived in the same building, though in the basement.
When she said she thought she might be pregnant, he assured her that
Lennie would give her an abortion. Later she told him that she had
only been kidding.

They found Friar in a bar. He had one hundred and twenty-two
dollars left and was drunk. They worked frantically to get him sober
for the film.

While Friar was editing the film and Yvette was away in Ste Agathe, Duddy had dinner with Mr. Calder, who revealed that he had just bought controlling interest in a factory just outside Montreal. Afterwards, Duddy phoned Cohen, offering him the contract to pick up the scrap weekly from Calder's factory. Cohen was doubtful that Duddy could make the arrangements with Calder, but they agreed on twelve-and-a-half percent commission if Duddy could get the deal.

Duddy's problems mounted. Yvette returned with the news that she needed two thousand dollars to close the deal on the second parcel of land; Friar's film for Seigal turned out to be hopeless; the film company was pressing for settlement of an outstanding account for nine hundred dollars; a car payment was due; the office and apartment rentals had to be seen to; Duddy's bank account was overdrawn by one-hundred and sixty-seven dollars. Then Virgil, with whom Duddy had made the deal for the pinball machines, arrived; he had ten machines ready to deliver at one hundred dollars each. Taking benzedrine pills to stay awake, Duddy decided to drive to Ste Agathe to try to sell the machines.

Commentary

Duddy's financial "empire" is facing a dangerous moment of crisis which drives Duddy to extremes of behaviour. In the beginning, after first seeing the land he wanted, he had been driven by his hysterical excitement to near collapse. The pace has not slowed for him. Now, he takes pills to drive himself even harder. The land is his one desire.

Chapter Thirteen

Summary

At a hotel in Ste Agathe, Virgil confessed to being an epileptic. His one desire was to fight for the rights of epileptics. Duddy, exhausted by the long, difficult drive, was unsympathetic.

Duddy sold all the pinball machines except one, getting an average price of two hundred and twenty-five dollars for them. He informed Yvette that he now had the money for the land, but ignored her reminder that he owed Virgil a thousand dollars. While Yvette and Virgil went to a movie, he visited his land. Unfortunately, in the winter cold and dark he became lost. When he finally got back to the hotel he was feverish again. But he did not forsake business. He phoned Friar to find out how he was succeeding in piecing together something presentable from the Seigal film, and he made deals with four hotels to supply them with movies one night a week.

Duddy offered Virgil a job driving to Ste Agathe to show the movies each week. He would be paid sixty dollars a week. There was one problem; he would have to have a truck. However, Duddy told him that he had the very vehicle for him, and could arrange to get it for one thousand dollars. Virgil was delighted. Yvette was not. She suspected the truth, that Duddy was obtaining the truck for less than a thousand dollars. Moreover, she was deeply disturbed to learn that Virgil was an epileptic; she was worried that he might have an accident, for she liked him. She and Duddy quarrelled bitterly, and Yvette did not return to work until Duddy informed Virgil that the truck would cost only seven hundred and fifty dollars.

In six months Duddy had obtained more than a third of the land he wanted.

Commentary

Duddy's indifference to those who show him most affection is clearly displayed. Virgil is an ingenuous young man who feels his physical affliction deeply. He is poor, having lost most of his savings in an unsuccessful pinball venture. Nevertheless, Duddy is prepared to exploit him, harnessing the last of Virgil's money to support Dudley Kane Enterprises. Duddy's treatment of Yvette is no better. She cannot return to her family because they do not approve of her relationship with Duddy, yet he blithely speaks of an abortion when she mentions the possibility of being pregnant.

Part Three

Chapter One

Summary

Duddy's winter was exceptionally prosperous and happy. He picked up a small profit from the Seigal movie and did well with three others. He travelled to Toronto to find out about making industrial films. On the distribution side he sometimes made a profit. He even got a paragraph in Mel West's column for his willingness to show movies free for charitable organizations.

Duddy's apartment became a gathering place for Bohemians. There was Blum the editor of the poetry magazine *Attack,* to which Virgil submitted poems who reminded Duddy of Cuckoo Kaplan; Bernie was always there; and a frequent visitor was the serious Hersh, a high school associate, who had given up his studies to become a writer. Hersh and Yvette warned Duddy that the people who came were only taking advantage of him and were actually laughing at him behind his back, but Duddy simply responded with a platitude: "Man does not live by bread alone." However, Yvette was glad to have Duddy at home, though she worried about what would happen when he had acquired all of the land and was faced with the enormous expense of development.

In addition, Duddy arranged the scrap deal with Mr. Calder for Cohen. Calder was displeased that Duddy should want to raise the question of a business deal with him, and they did not see one another again for a month.

Time became an obsession with Duddy as he launched on a relentless quest for self-improvement. He also insisted that Bernie get him a date with a Jewish girl, explaining that Yvette knew he could not marry her. However, the date was a disaster. Duddy was stiff and unnatural, and he offended the girl by asking her to tell her father that his mills made the best sweaters. Thus Duddy put the thought of marrying a rich Jewish girl out of his head for the moment. There was time for that; meanwhile, he could relax with Yvette.

Duddy was so busy he did not have much time for his family. However, he met Uncle Benjy by chance and was shocked at his thinness. Benjy explained that he had had an operation for an ulcer. However, Duddy learned the truth from Lennie; Benjy was dying, and Ida had left him. Duddy decided that he must go to the States to see Ida and tell her the truth about her husband.

Yvette arrived with the news that Friar had left and taken the cameras with him. He had asked her to marry him and had taken off when she had turned him down. Duddy angered Yvette by finding the whole affair amusing. In her anger she warned him ominously that all the deeds to the land were in her name.

Commentary

(1) Part of the tension in the plot of the novel derives from the suggestion that perhaps Duddy's career will end in tragedy through the treachery of Yvette. All of the titles to the land are in her name, since Duddy is still under age. Yvette, of course, does not adopt that

course of action, but suspense is created through the suggestion of that possibility.

(2) The chapter contains an amusing, satiric portrait of the career of the social-climbing Jew. Duddy is a crass materialist, and yet he has an unquenchable desire to be liked and respected. Thus, on the one hand he can offend the girl with whom Bernie has arranged a date by speaking gauchely of her father's business, and on the other hand he can try earnestly to impress her with his intellectual gifts by tiresomely discussing serious topics. That there are blind spots in Duddy's self-knowledge is painfully obvious.

(3) Nevertheless, we see that Duddy's compassion in family matters is infinite. Benjy and Duddy are not at all friendly, yet Duddy has no hesitation in deciding to bring Ida back to Montreal when he learns that his uncle is dying.

Chapter Two

Summary

Duddy had not seen Ida for twelve years. All he remembered of her was her association with perfume and suitcases and the unusual gifts she sent to their house while on her many travels. He found her with a young man in a seedy hotel. Her appearance shocked him; she was dressed foolishly in a Mexican costume and wore too much makeup. She declared that Benjy's cancer was only psychosomatic, a trick to make her feel guilty. It was the same, she said, when he had told his father that he was impotent. Actually, she was the one who could not have children and Benjy had asumed the blame just to make her feel more guilty. Duddy was embarrassed by her appearance and by her foolish talk, but he managed to get her to Montreal.

Uncle Benjy summoned Duddy to his house three days later. He told his nephew that he had known he was dying ever since leaving the hospital. Now he wanted to put his affairs in order. He offered Duddy fifty percent of his estate if he would run the factory for him. But Duddy spurned the offer. He confronted Benjy with the fact that he had always showered his favours on Lennie and had, in Duddy's eyes, treated Duddy badly at the factory. Benjy retorted that he could not stand Duddy because he was what he detested, a Jew-boy on the make. However, Duddy's passionate portrayal of his difficulties and ambitions led Benjy to see a new side to the boy. He realized with surprise that Duddy was the only relative who had not come to him for handouts and he expressed his regret that he had not seen in Duddy what his grandfather had seen. Unfortunately no real reconciliation took place. Duddy fled the room after screaming to the doctor that he must not let Benjy die.

Commentary

The confrontation between Benjy and Duddy is a crucial scene in the novel. It portrays clearly the dual aspect of Duddy's personality. On the one hand, it is easy to dismiss Duddy in the way that Benjy has dismissed him, as a contemptuous example of a Jew-boy on the make, a crass and ignorant materialist whose ambitions make a mockery of his race. On the other hand, however, Benjy has come to see more. He has realized for the first time the value of the decisiveness and independence at the heart of the restless ambition. Thus, though some might dismiss Duddy as a foolish figure, Benjy has at last seen the fiery individuality and talent underlying the ambition. His new insight is a source of unquenchable regret.

Chapter Three

Summary

Yvette brought the news that Virgil had had a bad accident with the truck. His spine was broken; he had lost all sensation and control below the waist and would be in a wheelchair for the rest of his life. Duddy's first reaction was to curse his bad luck when everything was going so well. Yvette, however, was angry with Duddy for getting Virgil to drive the truck in the first place. He had always treated Virgil as a possession, she remonstrated, and he treated her in the same way. A bitter quarrel ensued, with the result that Yvette stated that she was moving to Ste Agathe with Virgil. She would get a job and look after him; they did not need Duddy. Their parting was violent and bitter.

Commentary

The chapter reveals only the monstrous side of Duddy Kravitz. He has no real feeling for Virgil, whose survival is an embarrassment, an uncomfortable source of guilt. Thus, the two people who had helped Duddy and had genuine affection for him are cast aside.

Chapter Four

Summary

Duddy's film shows kept him working frantically, and that summer his appearance and his nerves suffered. He looked for fights everywhere and lost three clients. Although Reyburn, Friar's replacement, was good, Duddy did not enjoy working with him; he missed Friar's craziness.

One night he ran into Cuckoo Kaplan in Ste Agathe, and Duddy insulted the comedian, informing him that he lacked talent. In response, Cuckoo declared that he had heard that Duddy had changed. He went on to say that Yvette was in Ste Agathe looking after Virgil, and that rumour had it that Duddy had taken them for every cent they had. Also, Irwin was now a lawyer and was apparently advising Virgil to sue Duddy. Duddy shoved Cuckoo aside and left.

On returning to Montreal, Duddy wrote a long letter to Hersh, explaining how much he loved and missed Yvette and stating that he was on the brink of suicide. He then sealed it in an envelope addressed to Yvette. He wrote a second letter to Yvette saying that the letter to Hersh had been sent to her by mistake and asking her not to read it. Duddy's ruse did not work; Yvette returned both letters unopened.

Benjy died and Duddy attended the funeral. His clients in the resorts had heard of the death and did not expect him with the movies, but they were annoyed that he did not even phone them.

On the brink of a nervous breakdown, he stayed in bed for two days, during which time he was troubled by wild dreams. A messenger bearing a letter written by Uncle Benjy woke him. Duddy cast the letter aside. Mr. Calder also wanted to see him. Duddy met Calder, but their meeting was unsatisfactory. Duddy said that he wasn't feeling well and went home.

Duddy went to see Hersh, who was leaving for Europe next week. Hersh advised Duddy, who was obviously troubled by guilt feelings over the death of Mr. MacPherson's wife, to see a doctor.

Commentary

Duddy is in the throes of a psychological crisis caused in part by the previous confrontation with his Uncle Benjy. At that time, his true feelings had found expression. He had admitted his craving for affection and his awareness of what others thought of him. Coupled with the knowledge of his uncle's approaching death, these admissions brought Duddy a sense of futility. In addition, he was deeply troubled by feelings of guilt in connection with both Mrs. MacPherson and Virgil. His reaction was to drive himself harder, but the exultation was gone. He neglected himself and became unbearably irritable even with clients. It is clear that at this point Duddy is feeling his loneliness acutely. He has no friends, and Yvette will not even communicate with him. His neglected business only adds to the burden.

Chapter Five

Summary

Financial disaster struck. Duddy was so unreliable that no one wanted him to show movies, and he was inundated with bills. On his lawyer's advice, Duddy declared bankruptcy.

To keep himself going, he drove his father's cab at night. On one occasion, Mr. Cohen was a fare and he insisted on Duddy coming home with him. Cohen wanted to know all that had happened. Under the influence of liquor, he assured Duddy that he would help. He brushed aside Duddy's feelings of guilt about Virgil, whom he dismissed as a *goy*. Besides, he declared, he too had had his problems. His partner had gone to prison only because Mr. Cohen, who should have gone to prison, had been smarter, and a worker had once been killed because of faulty machinery. Duddy, he insisted, must go on, in spite of his troubles.

Duddy did not improve. He took his fathers cab on a full shift and added another shift with another cab in order to pay the rent. He lost weight and passed his spare time playing games with himself.

He received a letter from Virgil, who assumed that Duddy had not been to see him because he was angry over the accident. He asked Duddy to visit Ste Agathe and enclosed copies of a mimeographed magazine he was publishing.

Commentary

It is obvious at this point that Duddy has a choice to make. He can follow Mr. Cohen's urgings and persist in his ambitions for material success. That will involve indifference to the feelings of others who might be sacrificed to those ambitions. The second choice is more difficult to discern. However, it would seem to involve some modification of the material goals. Duddy, of course, has to find a way out of his present financial difficulties, but that does not necessarily involve the former relentless pursuit of success. The letter from Virgil almost seems to be a reminder of the more human choice available to Duddy.

Chapter Six

Summary

Chapter Six is devoted entirely to one issue of The Crusader which is "The Only Magazine in the World Published By Epileptics For Epileptics."

Chapter Seven

Summary

When Yvette learned that Duddy had gone into bankruptcy, she invited him to stay with Virgil and her in Ste Agathe. In the days following, Duddy seemed to relax completely. He welcomed the thought that perhaps everyone would forget him. Then he read Benjy's letter. His uncle had left Duddy the house in Montreal, but it could not be sold. Benjy also warned Duddy that he was two people: "a scheming little bastard" and a "fine, intelligent boy." Soon, Benjy wrote, Duddy would be of age, and he must decide which kind of man he was to be. The letter impelled Duddy to revisit his property. He exulted in the beauty and peace, though he noticed that a woman and a man using two canes had recently been on the land.

On returning, Yvette informed him that the rest of the land was up for sale and that he would need forty-five hundred to secure it. At first Duddy was not interested, and Yvette was delighted that after his nervous collapse he was not going to start running again. Then he read in the newspaper that Dingleman had been declared to be linked with New York dope smuggling. Immediately he phoned Lennie to ask what heroin was like and asked him to run some tests on some powder he had. Following the call, he declared his intention of returning to Montreal, saying that he would have money in no time, for his luck had changed.

Commentary

Benjy's letter is of vital importance, for it is the most explicit statement in the novel of Duddy's predicament. He is indeed two people, the one callous and grasping, the other intelligent and compassionate. The latter side of his nature had seemed to win out after his nervous breakdown, and there seemed to be every chance for Duddy to become the kind of person his grandfather had discerned him to be. But the struggle was only to begin again. The news of the Boy Wonder's misfortune had triggered Duddy's acquisitive instincts and made him ready and eager to compete once more.

Part Four

Chapter One

Summary

Duddy saw Dingleman and attempted to force the Boy Wonder to make him a loan of forty-five hundred dollars, but was met by refusal. Dingleman was not concerned about Duddy's telling of what the coffee can contained on the trip from New York; after all, he explained, Duddy had crossed the border with the suitcase. Moreover, Dingleman knew about the pinball machines that had crossed the border illegally.

Duddy next approached Mr. Cohen, remembering the earlier offer of help. Cohen was sober and refused help. The most he would do was to lend Duddy one thousand dollars in return for help in getting the contract for the rest of Mr. Calder's scrap.

A long-distance call to Aunt Ida proved fruitless. She was in Nice with a boy friend and asked Duddy to see the lawyer about getting her next cheque sent to her immediately.

At home, Lennie broached the matter of Duddy's needing money with Max. After blustering, Max finally agreed, unwillingly, to lend Duddy a thousand dollars.

There was still twenty-two hundred dollars to find, but Duddy sent the money he had to Yvette, with the assurance that he would find the rest in time.

When Yvette and Virgil arrived to live in Montreal, they discovered a moving van at Uncle Benjy's house. Duddy had sold the contents, including antiques and the library, for seven hundred and fifty dollars. His explanation was simple: "My uncle's dead, I've got to go on living."

Mr. Calder was unhelpful. He was offended that Duddy, whom he regarded as a friend, should ask him for money.

Suddenly, Duddy thought of Virgil. Where had all the money come from to pay his hospital bills? Where had Yvette obtained the initial three hundred dollars she had placed as a deposit on the last land? Feeling sure that Virgil must have money, Duddy tried to persuade him to lend some. Virgil was upset and uncomfortable, but nonetheless firm. He could not use his money; Yvette had instructed him to keep it for a time of need. However, when Virgil and Yvette went out for a stroll, Duddy found Virgil's passbook. He forged a check and deposited it in his own account. Afterwards he announced gleefully that he had the money and sent Yvette to Ste Agathe to close the deal.

On her return, he had her sign all of the deeds over to his father. It was just a legal formality, he insisted, because he himself was still under age, but she refused to join in his toast to success.

When they returned to the house, Virgil was lying on the floor; he had had a fit. Duddy, sensing the reason for the seizure, ran out.

Commentary

It is clear that Duddy has made his choice. He has re-embarked upon the activities that previously ruined his health and lost him his friends. Consequently, his actions are little short of monstrous. In effect he desecrates the legacy of the house left to him by Benjy, though it had been built and furnished for Benjy's sons. Further, he has cynically and calculatedly used Virgil to further his own schemes, caring little that the man who regarded him as a friend is a virtually helpless cripple.

Duddy has achieved his goal; he now possesses the land of which he had dreamed. Perhaps unwittingly, Duddy has also achieved something else; he has become the kind of person against whom his Uncle Benjy had warned him.

Chapter Two

Summary

Duddy, Max, Lennie and Simcha drove out to see the land. Duddy was ecstatic and proud, but he was puzzled by his grandfather's lack of enthusiasm.

While they were there, Jerry Dingleman and Linda approached. The Boy Wonder congratulated Duddy and offered to share in the development of the land. But Duddy savoured every moment of his triumph. He abused Dingleman and ordered him off the land.

Returning home, Simcha declared that he did not want any part of the land. Yvette had visited him and told him of Duddy's forging the cheque. He would have no part of it. Lennie was astonished to see that his grandfather was weeping.

Duddy sought out Yvette and remonstrated with her for going to Simcha, the one person he respected. She retorted that she had wanted to hurt him as much as possible. Indeed, if she had her way she would sue him for the forgery, but Virgil simply wanted to be left alone. Neither of them wanted to see Duddy again. As she left, he shouted that she would come crawling back to him.

Back at Lou's Bagel & Lox Bar, Max was regaling his listeners with his story of Duddy and his achievement. Now, unconcerned by Duddy's immoral actions, he was proudly declaring that he knew that his son would be a great success. Duddy was reluctant to join the gathering and with embarrassment asked for his fare home. However, he was stopped by a waiter who asked him if he was really the Mr. Kravitz who had bought all of the land. In that case, he said, his credit was good. Duddy's response was to be overcome with great joy. He seized his father, crying out, "You see. You see."

Commentary

Duddy has achieved what he wanted. In a sense, that achievement has two aspects. In the first place, he had obtained the land he had desired; in the second place, however, he had also achieved what he had also always wanted . . . his father's approval. Duddy was now a local celebrity, and Max was talking of Duddy in the same way that he used to talk about the Boy Wonder. Yet there is a third achievement of which Duddy is not conscious at this moment. As his final joy shows, he has cast behind him the injustice he has done to Yvette and to Virgil; he has become the kind of person Uncle Benjy had unhappily seen in him from the beginning.

CHARACTERS

John Alexander MacPherson

Mr. MacPherson, a teacher of history at Fletcher's Field High School, had come to the school in 1927 as "a tight-lipped young Scot with a red fussy face." His original dreams for his career had been noble, for he had hoped that his work would be "blessed with charity and achievement." He had also looked forward hopefully to the days of the future when former students would return to visit him to enjoy nostalgic gatherings at his home. Further, he was one of the few teachers who refused to use the strap.

However, by 1947 it was clear that Mr. MacPherson's dreams were never to come true. Now, as he looked at the school he "felt nothing about the building." Though many of his former students had gone on to make distinguished careers for themselves, there were no pleasant reunions at his home. Even his refusal to use the strap was now only an empty gesture born of stubborn egotism:

> Long ago Mr. MacPherson had vowed never to strap a boy. The principle itself, like the dream of taking Jenny on a trip to Europe, keeping up with the latest educational books, or saving to buy a house, was dead. But his refusal to strap was still of the greatest consequence to Mr. MacPherson. 'There,' they'd say, 'goes the only teacher in FFHS who has never strapped a boy.' That he no longer believed in not-strapping was beside the point. As long as he refused to do it Mr. MacPherson felt that he would always land safely. There would be no crack-up. He would survive.
>
> (p. 17)

Thus, what he did no longer moved or inspired him. We can see the extent to which his enthusiasm has withered in the fact that when he thinks of Shelley's "Ode to the West Wind," only two dry facts spring into his mind – the page number on which the poem appeared in *Highroads to Reading,* and the fact of its central idea being "the poet's dedication to a free and natural spirit" (p. 7). This last point is, of course, pointedly ironic, for there was no spirit less free and natural than John Alexander MacPherson.

The visible signs of MacPherson's degeneration as a teacher and as a man showed in his appearance and his habits. By 1947, "his

Characters are discussed in order of their appearance in the novel.

face seemed more bitingly angry and the curly black hair had greyed." He had also become a heavy drinker. His drinking had not yet become a problem, as it was clearly to be after his wife's death, but in combination with his own sense of failure it did contribute to his ineffectiveness as a human being. Thus, for example, when he decided to take home a box of chocolates for his wife (chapter two), he first visited the Pines Tavern. Once there, he continually postponed the task of buying the chocolates, so engrossed was he in reflecting on his problems. The result was that he returned home without buying the gift for Jenny.

It is difficult to discern the causes of MacPherson's deterioration. Perhaps, in the first place, his dreams had been too naively idealistic in not recognizing the hard facts of human nature. Schoolboys – alas! – are not always noble creatures. MacPherson obviously found that fact hard to face. He would, for example, be frustrated to find that not strapping could be interpreted not as a sign of belief in human goodness, but as a sign of weakness. Yet this is precisely the challenging interpretation Duddy flung at MacPherson (p. 12). Further, Mr. MacPherson's idea of giving merit cards to deserving students was torpedoed by Jerry Dingleman, who collected cards from other boys by gambling. Perhaps also, Mr. MacPherson's failure was due to his inability to change with the changing times. He recognized and rewarded very formal, conservative values: high examination results, good behaviour, and neat writing. But between 1927 and 1947 the social environment of the school had changed and was still changing radically. At one time, most Jewish boys who had gone to high school in Montreal had attended Fletcher's Field. Now the area was changing. More affluent Jews moved to the more prosperous district of Outremont, and Europeans were gradually moving into the school area. Moreover, Duddy's society, located, as it were, midway between the slums and the middle class, tended to value material things gained by the wits rather than distinction earned through scholarship. That is why the Boy Wonder was the folk hero of the group. To be a successful teacher, MacPherson would have had to relate much more to the real concerns of the students before him.

Of course, MacPherson's situation reached critical proportions with the illness of his wife, Jenny. That illness reinforced his sense of failure because he felt that he could not do what was needed to help her. Consequently, when she became ill in the night MacPherson did not call the doctor, who would only prescribe the impossible remedy of a month's rest in the mountains. MacPherson simply watched over her in her illness, spending the lonely night hours in despair and anxiety. He was, in fact, an almost totally defeated man at this stage. He admitted that defeat to himself on the night of Jenny's death, when he was returning home from the party given by Herbert Shields:

> Once in the taxi he recalled how Herbert had introduced him to a group of strangers. 'I want you to shake the hand of the most brilliant student of our class at McGill. He could have been a success at anything he wanted. Instead he's devoted his life to teaching.' It was clear that they still took him for the freshly scrubbed idealist who had left McGill twenty years ago. They had no idea that he was exhausted, bitter, and drained, and that given the chance to choose again he would never become a teacher.
>
> (p. 31)

The end came for MacPherson with the death of Jenny. The death itself was almost something of a relief, partly perhaps because it was the end of long, exhausting, anxious months of vigil, but partly also because it meant the end of the guilt he undoubtedly felt at not being able to provide more adequately for the wife whom he had loved so truly. However true all of that may have been, there can be little doubt that it was the manner of Jenny's death which disturbed MacPherson equally deeply. Jenny had died through the foolish prank of Duddy, who had delivered one of his obscene phone calls late in the night. To an idealist, no matter how faded the ideals had become, the grossness of such human folly must have been profoundly shocking. The results – the increased drinking, the indiscriminate strapping, the neglect of duty, the blundering confrontations with students, the mental collapse – came inexorably.

Thus, though Mr. MacPherson is obviously a minor character in the novel and never appears beyond part one, his role in the novel is important. In the first place, of course, his presence helps to underline the nature of the central figure, Duddy Kravitz. In Duddy's relationship with MacPherson, we see the worst aspects of Duddy, who is shown to be rude, uncooperative, disrespectful, unfeeling and vindictive. The central character, we begin to understand, is no conventional hero, but rather an anti hero. Further, the relationship emphasizes one of the themes of the novel, which might be expressed as the clash between idealism and practical materialism: MacPherson embodies the former attitude, and Duddy embodies the latter. Distasteful though it may be, practical materialism often wins the victory. MacPherson has seen that fact clearly. That is why he feels acutely his sense of failure in his encounter with Herbert Shields.

More important, that is why MacPherson utters his prophetic words to Duddy: "You'll go far, Kravitz. You're going to go very far" (p. 40). In his hour of defeat, the teacher has recognized that in the conflict between idealism and less noble attitudes, the battle is often won by the amoral persistence and ingenuity of practical materialism. The battle is, in a sense, the battle which Duddy is to wage throughout the novel. Thus it is by no means incongruous that a novel about Duddy should begin with the apparently incongruous figure of John Alexander MacPherson.

Duddy Kravitz

The reader's first encounter with Duddy offers some clues as to the nature of the hero:

> Duddy Kravitz was a small, narrow-chested boy of fifteen with a thin face. His black eyes were ringed with dark circles and his pale, bony cheeks were criss-crossed with scratches as he shaved twice daily in his attempt to encourage a beard.
>
> (p. 9)

There are two important aspects of Duddy in this description. On the one hand, there is the feeling of pathos which he arouses. On the other hand, there is, even at the age of fifteen, the desire to be something other than he is.

Duddy is frequently, throughout the novel, presented as a rather pathetic figure. Max's treatment of his younger son emphasizes this attitude. For example, when Duddy meets his father at Eddy's Cigar & Soda, Max declares foolishly, "Duddy's a dope like me" (p. 22). Further, Duddy constantly seeks from Max the kind of paternal affection which is never granted. Thus, on returning to Montreal from Ste Agathe, Duddy embraces his father warmly, but Max pushes the boy off with some embarrassment (part two, chapter one). At the same time, he asks why Max has not replied to his letters. Max protests that he is "not one for the letters," but Duddy could not help remembering that when Lennie had been away at camp, Max had written every week and had visited his older son twice (p. 105). It is clear that while Max may frequently utter platitudes about family solidarity, his real concern is for Lennie. Duddy fares little better at the hands of his other relatives. Lennie is not really interested in the welfare of his younger brother. In chapter three, part one, Duddy attempts to interest Lennie in the events of the day at school. Lennie is preoccupied with his studies. Duddy again tries to evoke some response. He declares that Lennie does not need to worry about college fees; he will get a job as a waiter and give all his tips to Lennie. Moved by feelings of guilt, Lennie invites Duddy to the movies on Saturday afternoon, but the invitation is not genuine. Lennie knows that on Saturday morning he will regret the invitation. Uncle Benjy grants Duddy no better treatment. He "did not like Duddy on sight" (p. 61). He interpreted the boy's appearance in the worst possible way:

> . . . The thin crafty face, the quick black eyes and the restlessness, the blackheads and the oily skin, the perpetual fidgeting, the grin so shrewd and knowing, all made a bad impression on Uncle Benjy.
>
> (p. 61)

To Benjy, Duddy is the epitome of the *pusherke* — "A liitle Jew-boy on the make. Guys like you make me sick and ashamed" (p. 242). Unfortunately, the uncle's recognition of different qualities in the boy comes far too late to do either of them any good. Of the relatives, then, only the grandfather, Simcha recognizes the innate possibilities for good in Duddy. It is ironic, therefore, that Simcha's words to seven-year-old Duddy — "A man without land is nobody" — are the very words that lead to the destruction of that potential goodness in Duddy. The pathos inherent in Duddy's obvious craving for warmth and affection is only increased by the fact that his mother is dead. Thus, isolated even in the midst of his family, he frequently wonders about his mother. The main concern of Duddy's wondering is significant:

> There was a picture in the living-room of Max and Minnie on their wedding day. He wore a top hat and her face was in the shadow of a white veil. But her smile was tender, forgiving. It looked to Duddy as if she had probably used to laugh a lot. He could remember her laugh, come to think of it. Something rolling, turning over dark and deep and endless, and with it hugs and gooey kisses and a whiff of onions. He remembered too that Max had held him pinned down to the bed once, saying over and over again, 'Easy, kid, easy,' while Minnie had applied argyrol drops to his nose. *Once more Duddy was tempted to ask his father if Minnie had liked him, but he couldn't bring himself to risk it.*
>
> (p. 129, italics added)

The last sentence is particularly significant, for it is a clue to the meaning of the pathos associated with Duddy. The pathos is not simply an ingredient which helps Richler to persuade the reader to have some sympathy for this strange hero. The pathos brings sharply into focus Duddy's main struggle, which is to find himself, to discover his identity as a person.

The real self is not just an inert element lying within the self and awaiting discovery. It is something much more dynamic which, in part, can only be known in relationship with others. Self-knowledge involves relationship. Paradoxically, by turning the eyes outward — that is, by entering into relationships — one is able to see more clearly the inner reality of one's own being. Tragically, Duddy is not granted the opportunity for the kinds of relationships which would bring him illumination and enlightenment. Thus, uncertain of others, he does not know himself. Consequently, though wanting to know whether his mother liked him, he does not dare to ask the question. If the answer were negative, his worst fears about his worth as a person would be confirmed, since he was already acutely aware of his low value in the estimation of Max, Benjy and Lennie.

This insight helps to explain the nature of the novel. It is, we see, a story of initiation. Duddy must make the journey from boyhood to manhood, a journey which involves the discovery of the nature of the self. On the one hand, there is for Duddy that aspect of the self which is warm, human and compassionate. He wants to love and be loved. Thus, on first meeting Yvette he was "surprised and flattered to discover that anyone cared enough to watch him closely" (p. 92). On the other hand, however, there is that aspect of the self which has been forged by the rejection suffered at the hands of others. This is the aspect which drives Duddy to become someone other than he is at the moment. Consequently, as a boy he cannot wait to be a man (he shaves frantically and precociously to encourage a beard), thinking that his identity as a human being will be found in a new role. His search for identity becomes a concentration upon *getting* rather than *being*. He falsely concludes that his self lies in external things, and so he constantly looks for some kind of objective reality which will make his identity unmistakable. That is why he is almost hysterical on discovering the land at Ste Agathe. A man without land, he remembers, is nothing. He has found the land he wants. Now the acquiring of the land will lead to the acquisition of identity. That Duddy's choice of the road to identity is wrong is obvious. His choice leads to pain for others, and his success at the end has a hollow quality. His apprenticeship is a failure in that at crucial moments he fails to distinguish between human qualities and material things. Uncle Benjy tried finally to explain to Duddy the significance of what was happening:

There's more to you than mere money-lust, Duddy, but I'm afraid for you. You're two people, that's why. The scheming little bastard I saw so easily and the fine, intelligent boy underneath that your grandfather, bless him, saw. But you're coming of age soon and you'll have to choose. A boy can be two, three, four potential people, but a man is only one. He murders the others.

There's a brute inside you, Duddel – a regular behemoth – and this being such a hard world it would be the easiest thing for you to let it overpower you.

(p. 279)

But the attempt failed; Duddy's response was to sell the houseful of furniture that Benjy left. Duddy's justification for the act was simple and cynical: "My uncle's dead, I've got to go on living" (p. 296). Rejected by the people whom he respected, Duddy has sought and found his identity in things. At the end, it is Simcha who recognizes the human failure contained in the material success:

'I can see what you have planned for me, Duddel. You'll be good to me. You'd give me everything I wanted. And that would settle your conscience when you went out to swindle others.'

(p. 312)

The initiation theme is enriched by the innocence/experience aspect of Duddy's progress. Thus, the suggestion earlier in these notes (see the autobiographical section on Richler) of some similarity between Duddy and Huckleberry Finn is not trivial. Huck was an innocent abroad in the world, a young man with basic human responses, whose journey on the Mississippi became a symbolic life-journey in which the real state of the world and the true nature of men came to be recognized. Huck's naiveté or innocence not only got him into the situations in which he became embroiled, but also enabled him to make us see those situations more clearly and more objectively. Duddy is similarly an innocent abroad in the world. His naiveté makes him unable to understand Benjy's complicated reaction to the news of the worker's petty theft (p. 61–62). His naiveté leads to the agonies of his involvement with Irwin and Linda, whose cruelty is vividly revealed. His naiveté is the instrument whereby the pompous fraudulence of Friar is comically exposed. His naiveté casts into sharp focus the grossness of the Boy Wonder. His naiveté, indeed, gives Richler's novel its particular quality and texture. Without this innocence that is so intrinsically a quality of heroes in picaresque novels, the book might simply be a gloomy account of a minor human tragedy, in the manner of Theodore Dreiser. As it stands, however, the career of Duddy Kravitz, by giving us a sense of the comic absurdity which is so often so close to the heart of serious human experiences, holds up a far truer mirror to human life.

Hersh

Jacob Hersh is, at the beginning of *The Apprenticeship of Duddy Kravitz,* one of Duddy's classmates. However, he is quite different by nature. He reveals none of the ebullience and aggressiveness displayed by the other boys. When Duddy challenges MacPherson deliberately by lighting a cigarette outside the school (p. 9), Hersh makes a plea for moderate behaviour: "We're lucky to get Mac, so let's not take advantage like." Later, when MacPherson is confronted by a caricature of himself drawn on the blackboard, Hersh is mortified lest MacPherson should think him responsible for the drawing (p. 11). Thus Hersh emerges as a boy who desires only peace and order. His undoing, as far as his classmates were concerned, had been his participation in a Young Communist demonstration for cheaper chocolate bars. Such behaviour was unexpected coming from Hersh, and he had become "the butt of the class" (p. 11). However, Hersh was not cowardly, and he did speak frankly in opposing Duddy's attitudes: "You have to make everything dirty. Nothing's good for you, unless you can make it dirty" (p. 21).

Hersh was also different from Duddy in his scholastic accomplishments. On graduating from high school he had stood second in the province and had won a scholarship to McGill (p. 66). However, we learn later that he abandoned university in order to become a writer (p. 222). He had apparently done this not rashly and impetuously, but thoughtfully, in accordance with his strong principles: "There was no sense in staying on. I had no intention of becoming the apogee of the Jewish bourgeois dream. Namely a doctor or a lawyer" (p. 222–223). To further his new direction, Hersh has the intention of moving to Paris in the autumn.

Hersh thus emerges as an interesting character for two main reasons. First, he seems to have succeeded in achieving that sense of identity which has eluded Duddy. Hersh has found his vocation, a fact which is signalled by means of his physical change into manhood. Consequently, his presence would seem to emphasize further that Duddy's choice of goals in his search for identity is not an unavoidable choice. He has succeeded where, in a moral sense, Duddy has failed. The second interesting aspect is that Hersh seems to be an echo of Mordecai Richler himself, who also abandoned university and went to Paris to become a writer.

Hersh appears only briefly in *Duddy Kravitz*. However, the reader can follow up this character by reading *St. Urbain's Horseman,* for in that novel Hersh is the central character.

Lennie Kravitz

Lennie, the elder of the Kravitz brothers, is, unlike Duddy, a good student. Only two other Jewish students were admitted into the McGill medical school in his year, and a lot of people expected that he would be awarded a medal for scholarship (p. 169). As a result of his ability, Lennie had long been Uncle Benjy's favourite:

> They still shared the same bedroom. Duddy's side was thick with pennants and airplane models he had made and Lennie's side was laden with gifts from Uncle Benjy, the Books of Knowledge and the Harvard Classics. Lennie used to tell him about his talks with Uncle Benjy. 'He wants me to be the kind of doctor that's a helper to the poor. He's says I shouldn't worry if I can't get into medical school at McGill because of the anti-semitism there. Because he'll send me to Queens or Switzerland. Anywhere.
>
> (p. 164–165)

However, despite his ability, Lennie lacks the courage and tenacity of Duddy. He leans towards sham and hypocrisy. For example, he seems to be proud of his Jewishness; he joins the Hillel society (p. 165). Yet he is easily seduced by Sandra Calder's gentile group from Westmount and agrees to perform an abortion for Sandra (pp. 187 ff). In addition, earlier, when Lennie had begun to date the rich Jewish girl, Riva, he had pretended to be what he was not; he had never mentioned his brother, and he had used Uncle Benjy's address (p. 165). In some ways, he is very like his father. Like Max, he is given to mouthing platitudes: "Anatomy's the big killer." Like Max, he seems to have little genuine affection for Duddy; feeling guilty, he invites Duddy to the movies, and then immediately regrets the impulse (p. 20). It is scarcely surprising, then, that when real trouble appears with the Sandra Calder abortion, Lennie's response is to flee to Toronto. It is Duddy, contemptuously described by Lennie as greedy (p. 188), who solves the problem by confronting Mr. Calder. To his credit, Calder sees shrewdly through Duddy's explanation that Lennie could not come to Calder because Lennie is sensitive and subject to headaches (p. 197).

Though Lennie's future is in the end finally secured by a trust fund, Uncle Benjy does at last understand Lennie's shallowness in contrast to Duddy's independence:

'You don't want anything from me. Come to think of it, you're the only one in the family who never came here to ask for something. My God, it never occured to me before. You're the only one. Duddel, I've been unfair to you.'

'I can never tell if you're joking. There's such a tricky business in your voice, if you know what I mean?'

'I'm not joking. Lennie, your father, all of Ida's family, nobody has ever come to visit me without the hand outstretched. Except you. Now isn't that something?'

(p. 243)

Max Kravitz

Complete and utter shallowness is the mark of Max Kravitz's character. He is betrayed most obviously by the way he speaks, for what he says is liberally sprinkled with platitudes. One of the most vivid examples of his empty pomposity and blundering ignorance is his interview with Mr. Bush, the principal of Fletcher's Field. Max has arrived at the school to complain about Mr. MacPherson's late-night telephone call. His foolish, empty self-pride is comically apparent:

'You call me Max. I'm a simple man, Mr. Bush, a taxi driver. But a taxi driver, Mr. Bush, is a little like being a doctor. Night and day, rain or shine, I am at the service of John Q. Public. You'd be surprised at the things that come up in my life. Pregnant women to be rushed to the hospital, accidents, fights, and older men with fine reputations, if you'll pardon me, trying to have sexual relations with young girls in the back of my taxi. No, thank you. But, like I said, it is nothing for me to be called to an emergency in the middle of the night so, as you can well understand, I can't afford to have my sleep disturbed for nothing.'

(p. 38)

As usual, Max, in this scene, is betrayed by his own words. His righteous indignation and smug morality would be more credible, were he not a pimp for Josette.

Further, Max's shallowness is demonstrated just as clearly by his hero worship of Jerry Dingleman, the Boy Wonder. Dingleman is a criminal involved in drugs and gambling, yet Max's admiration for him is unequivocal: ". . . if the Boy Wonder knocked off his mother Max here is the guy who would find an excuse for him" (p. 23). Even when the Boy Wonder has been charged with criminal activities, Max's admiration is undimmed:

'Have you seen the paper,' he said. 'Boy, the Wonder's lined up the sharpest battery of legal-eagles in the country. He's playing it smart too. He's got Shubert – that's the brains of the outfit, I figure – and two bigshot *goys* for display. Aw, they'll wipe the floor with Cote.

(p. 292)

Not unexpectedly, however, when Duddy demonstrates that he can stand up to the Boy Wonder and that his star is in the ascendent, Max switches his allegiance swiftly. Previously he had been scornful of Duddy's enterprises; now, in the moment of Duddy's material triumph, he sits in the bar, telling the same exaggerated stories about his son that he had earlier told about Dingleman:

When Duddy finally returned to the store his father's back was to him. Max sat at a table piled high with sandwiches and surrounded by strangers. 'Even as a kid,' he said, sucking a sugar cube, 'way back there before he had begun to make his mark, my boy was a trouble-maker. He was born on the wrong side of the tracks with a rusty spoon in his mouth, so to speak, and the spark of rebellion in him. A motherless boy,' he said, pounding the table, 'but one who thrived on adversity, like Maxim Gorky or Eddy Cantor, if you're familiar with their histories. You could see from the day of his birth that he was slated for fame and fortune. A comer. Why I remember when he was still at FFHS they had a teacher there, an anti-semite of the anti-semites, a lush-head, and my boy was the one who led the fight against him and drove him out of the school. Just a skinny little fart he was at the time, a St Urbain Street boy, and he led a fearless campaign against this bastard MacPherson . . . '

(p. 315)

The foolishness of Max's narrative is evident to the reader, particularly in the account of the MacPherson incident, in which Duddy had certainly not acted as a courageous, religious leader, but rather as a callous and vindictive schoolboy whose irresponsible action had contributed to the death of an innocent human being.

In the end, Uncle Benjy's judgement of Max is probably the closest to the truth: "Max is not very bright" (p. 242). Only someone close to being a fool could remind a son of his debt of gratitude by declaring that he had missed Lux Theatre and the last game of the Little World Series when Duddy had had chickenpox as a child. Only someone close to being a fool could base his days so solidly on the power of platitudes: "I'm a simple man"; "Money is the root of all evil"; "When I lose my temper, I lose my temper"; "Anatomy's the killer".

It would be easy to take an overserious view of Max and to be horrified at the perverted influence which he obviously had over

Duddy, who in the end seems to surrender to Max's values. But that would be to overlook the comic nature of Max's irresponsibility. In the last analysis, he is the comic caricature of one kind of St. Urbain Street denizen — unsuccessful, yet living on fantasy, and ignorant, yet dramatic and compelling in his gift for fictitious narrative.

Simcha Kravitz

Simcha Kravitz, the father of Benjy and Max and the grandfather of Lennie and Duddy, came to Canada as an immigrant from Lodz at the turn of the century. His railway ticket took him only as far as Montreal, and that was as far as he had travelled in his new land. A shoemaker by trade, he was able to establish his own shop on St. Dominique Street three years after his arrival.

The key quality in his character is a kind of uncompromising integrity. Thus, though his marriage does not seem to have been a very happy one, no word of complaint escaped his lips, and he would allow no comment upon it (p. 45). In addition, his fellow immigrants regarded him as "a man of singular honesty and some wisdom." His shop became a kind of gathering place to which immigrants came for help, advice or reassurance. Simcha's stubborn integrity is nowhere more clearly shown than in the ending of the novel, when Duddy has at last acquired the land he sought so feverishly. He rejects Duddy's accomplishment, for he perceives that the moral cost of the acquisition has been too great:

'I can see what you have planned for me, Duddel. You'll be good to me. You'd give me everything I wanted. And that would settle your conscience when you went out to swindle others.'

(p. 312)

However, Simcha's very source of strength is also, in a sense, the source of his weakness. His fierce integrity seems to breed a kind of aloofness which others find cold. Some of his fellow immigrants resent him for his silent strength (p. 45). Moreover, when Benjy's marriage runs into trouble, Benjy does not feel that he can consult his father. His visits to Simcha become less frequent, and he lies to his father about being impotent.

Perhaps the main ingredient in Simcha's character is his idealism, which had over the years, however, become frustrated. Symbolic of this frustrated idealism is his attempt to grow vegetables. The soil is "gritty" and "hostile" (p. 45), but Simcha persists, even though every year "the corn came up scrawnier and the cucumbers yellowed before they ripened." Like Willie Loman in Arthur Miller's *Death of a Salesman,* his barren garden is his statement of his dreams, a statement which is negated by his experience. Nor had his family turned idealism into reality. Max, he stated flatly, was a fool (p. 48). Benjy, in his early years a delight to Simcha (p. 46), was, by his own confession, a disappointment as a man:

> . . . But there's something you ought to know about me. Every year of my life I have looked back on the man I was the year before – the things I did and said – and I was ashamed. All my life I've ridiculed others, it's true, but I was the most ridiculous figure of all, wasn't I?
>
> (p. 279)

Further, shrewd though he was, Simcha was to suffer similar disappointment with Duddy. He saw the "fine, intelligent boy" that was in Duddy (p. 279), but was later to be repelled by the "scheming little bastard" that Duddy proved to be.

In the end, it is probably Simcha's dreams which defeat both him and Duddy. His honesty is the major reason for his rejection of Duddy's gift of land. However, a minor reason may be that suggested by Dingleman in his vivid picture of the value that dreams, rather than reality, possessed for the old Jewish immigrants:

> . . . Sitting in their dark cramped ghetto corners they wrote the most mawkish, school-girlish stuff about green fields and sky. Terrible poetry, but touching when you consider the circumstances under which it was written. Your grandfather doesn't want any land. He wouldn't know what to do with it.
>
> (p. 310)

Finally – and ironically – Simcha's dreams start Duddy on the path of his destruction as a human being. He tells the seven-year-old Duddy, "A man without land is nobody." Duddy accepts the dictum without question. In fact, he ultimately does what Simcha is unable to bear: he turns the dream into reality. Thus the man of fierce integrity helped to create the man of acquisitive greed.

Benjamin Kravitz

Uncle Benjy is one of the more intriguing characters in *The Apprenticeship of Duddy Kravitz.*

On the one hand, we are faced with one judgement of Benjy which is delivered most forcefully by Jerry Dingleman: "I know your uncle,

Benjamin Kravitz. He's a childish man. I don't like him" (p. 141).
Benjy is at times presented as a ridiculous figure. "A short fat man
in enormous blue shorts with a golf ball pattern" (p. 58-59), he is
not respected by anyone. Thus, though he espouses socialist causes,
he gets along no better with communists than he does with capitalists.
Even his workers, whom he treats well, take advantage of him, as
Duddy discovers (p. 61).

Yet Benjy is not really a fool. He has become wealthy by his own
efforts:

> . . . He was a shrewd boy, intelligent and quick and without fear of
> the new country and he undoubtedly had, as Katansky put it, the
> golden touch. The fat teenage boy who ventured into the country to
> sell the farmers reams of cloth and boots and cutlery was, at twenty-
> six, the owner of a basement blouse factory.
>
> (p. 46)

However, the ability has been corroded by disappointment. His
unsuccessful marriage has changed him inexorably. Unable to bear
children, Ida surrendered to liquor and other men. Compassionately,
Benjy shouldered the blame, declaring his own impotence (p. 237).
His love for his wife continued, hopeless and pathetic:

> Always, before going to sleep, he kissed Ida on the forehead. Some-
> times, more drunken times, he would hold her close, his head squeezed
> against her breasts, and she would waken dizzy and afraid. He never
> knew that. She made sure he never realized that her sleep had been
> disturbed. But come morning Ida would be gone again.
>
> (p. 59)

This disappointment overflowed into the rest of his life, so that he
was even bored by the socialist magazines he read. Thus his disappointment and boredom led him to drink heavily.

Towards the end of his life, Benjy sees his own situation very
clearly. With considerable astonishment, he begins to see in Duddy
something of himself. Thus his last letter to Duddy is at once moving
and revealing:

> You lousy, intelligent people, that's what you said to me, and I
> haven't forgotten. I wasn't good to you, it's true. I never took time.
> I think I didn't like you because you're a throwback, Duddel. I'd look
> at you and remember my own days as a hungry salesman in the
> mountains and how I struggled for my first little factory. I'd look at
> you and see a busy, conniving little yid, and I was wrong because
> there was more, much more. But there's something you ought to know
> about me. Every year of my life I have looked back on the man I was

the year before – the things I did and said – and I was ashamed. All my life I've ridiculed others, it's true, but I was the most ridiculous figure of all, wasn't I?

(p. 278–279)

In his last moments, Benjy understands the emptiness of his accomplishments. The magnificent house on Mount Royal, furnished so splendidly for his descendants, is merely a house haunted by dreams of what might have been. Now, he will not be sorry to die (p. 242).

It is clear that Benjy offers a curious parallel to Duddy. Like Duddy, Benjy had in his early years been hungry for material success. Possessed of "the golden touch," he had prospered. But the prosperity did not bring happiness. The prosperity could not heal the defective relationship with Ida. What was left was depressing: "We eat each other up, Duddel. That's life" (p. 242). Consequently, in his moment of revelation, Benjy perceives the danger for Duddy and seeks earnestly to warn his nephew:

There's more to you than mere money-lust, Duddy, but I'm afraid for you. You're two people, that's why. The scheming little bastard I saw so easily and the fine, intelligent boy underneath that your grandfather, bless him, saw. But you're coming of age soon and you'll have to choose. A boy can be two, three, four potential people, but a man is only one. He murders the others.

There's a brute inside you, Duddel – a regular behemoth – and this being such a hard world it would be the easiest thing to let it overpower you. Don't, Duddel.

(p. 279)

Tragically for Duddy, Benjy's advice is ignored.

Yvette Durelle

Yvette is a French-Canadian girl with "black hair and large black eyes" (p. 97). When she first encounters Duddy, she is the second-floor chambermaid at Rubin's hotel in Ste Agathe.

She is an important figure in the story of Duddy Kravitz. From the beginning, she was attracted to Duddy; in Cuckoo Kaplan's crude terminology, she "had a real lust" for Duddy (p. 81). In reality, she is probably much more drawn by Duddy's loneliness. She has noticed his frantic, restless behaviour and taken note of the fact that he is extremely thin because of his hard work (pp. 92–93). Thus, when Duddy is at his loneliest, following the loss of his money in the roulette game, she is the person who offers him solace. She allows Duddy to make love to her (p. 92). She is never untrue to that love for Duddy until, in the end, his monstrous treatment of Virgil drives her to tell the whole sordid story to Simcha.

Though Duddy does not realize it, Yvette's genuine love is actually what he needs to become the man Simcha had seen in him. True love is a mature expression of complete sharing by two people who know themselves sufficiently well to engage in a total commitment of aspirations and emotions. It is the kind of sharing that cannot be experienced by two objects or by one person and one object. The relationship must truly be an "I-Thou" relationship, in which there is a mutual desire to share on the deepest personal level. Duddy is incapable of such mutual giving. His ambitions consume his being, so that the sensitive, intelligent, warm aspects of his personality are overlaid by the greed and materialism. Thus, Duddy's treatment of Yvette is crude, careless and callous. When he sees the land he wants to buy, he is completely indifferent to her. He acts as though he were alone (p. 98). After they have made love again (p. 100), he feels good, not because of her affection, but because of his excitement over the land. Moreover, blind to her feelings, he explains that he is too young to marry and, in any event, might have to marry a rich woman if he can find one (p. 101). Thus Yvette becomes an important instrument whereby the monstrous side of Duddy's nature is clearly revealed. She becomes, to him, an item of convenience. Consequently, she serves to gratify his lust (pp. 191–192) and to be his intermediary in the purchase of the land. The fact that she has been cast out by her family for her relationship with Duddy (pp. 217–218) means nothing to Duddy.

Yvette has those human qualities of compassion and tenderness which Duddy lacks. She is angry at Duddy's device for swindling Virgil out of the money owed for the pinball machines. She is appalled at Duddy's cynical employment of Virgil as a driver in view of his epilepsy. She is finally totally alienated by Duddy's stealing of the money in Virgil's bank account. Virgil has aroused in her the same sense of compassion that she had once felt for Duddy. Thus, though she has no real obligation to Virgil, she accepts full responsibility for him when he is paralyzed. She takes him to Ste Agathe, where she obtains work as a lawyer's private secretary in order to provide for both of them.

With Yvette, Duddy might have found the human identity he sought. At one point (pp. 281ff), it appears that she might be successful in her endeavour to save him from himself. Duddy declares that he is not interested in buying any more land, and

Yvette is relieved. However, Duddy is irrepressible. He starts running again. The break between them is total (pp. 312–315).

Apart from her function as a foil for Duddy, Yvette does not emerge as a vital character. We learn little of her appearance; her surname is mentioned only once; her family remains shadowy; and her ideas and activities apart from Duddy receive scant attention.

Irwin Shubert

Irwin, a "tall bronzed boy with curly black hair" (p. 68), is the nineteen-year-old son of one of the most famous criminal lawyers in Quebec. He is presented as an utterly repellant personality, without any redeeming qualities.

In his treatment of Duddy at Rubin's hotel (part one, chapters eleven, twelve and thirteen), he shows himself to be envious, vindictive, hypocritical and cruel. Jealous of Duddy's efficiency and conscientiousness as a waiter, Irwin turns the other boys against him, declaring that "it's the cretinous little money-grubbers like Kravitz that cause anti-semitism" (p. 68). Further, he plants the suspicion that Duddy has been stealing (p. 69); he is without doubt responsible for the disgusting trick with the bottle of Scotch (p. 70); and he masterminds the scheme to rob Duddy of his money in the roulette game. Yet, for all his cleverness, Irwin is a hypocrite. Said to be even more brilliant than his father, he possesses several books and poses as a serious student. However, Duddy shatters the pose when, in the middle of the night, he discovers Irwin poring over a medical book and masturbating.

Duddy is not the only victim of Irwin's unattractive capabilities. The pathetic comedian, Cuckoo Kaplan, has been lured to a bar one night on the promise of being introduced to an interested producer, only to be left responsible for Irwin's large bar bill. Later, Irwin exercises his talents upon Lennie. Fawning upon the rich, gentile crowd with whom he is associating, Irwin deliberately introduces Lennie into the group in order to oblige him to perform an abortion for Sandra Calder. It is not unfitting that when the abortion is attempted, Irwin is the one who loses his nerve and telephones Dr. Westcott (p. 188).

The portrait of Irwin, like many of the portraits in the novel, is barely more than a caricature. However, he makes two interesting contributions to the novel. First, his successful attempt to isolate Duddy at Rubin's hotel actually brings more money to Duddy and also propels Duddy into the relationship with Yvette which leads to the finding of the land about which Duddy has dreamed. Second, Irwin's involvement with Lennie leads to Duddy's acquaintance with Mr. Calder.

Linda Rubin

Linda is the only daughter of the owner of the Hotel Lac Des Sables. The description of her is typical of that of the spoiled, vain rich girl:

> . . . Linda was something else. Soft, curvy, and nifty enough for one of those snazzy fashion magazines, she seemed just about the most assured girl Duddy had ever met. She had been to Mexico and New York and sometimes she used words that made Duddy blush. Her cigarette holder, acquired on a trip to Europe, was made of real elephant tusk. At night in the recreation hall she seldom danced but usually sat at the bar joking with Irwin and Paddy and other favourites. Every afternoon she went riding and Duddy had often seen her starting down the dirt road to the stables, beating her whip against her boot.
>
> (p. 81)

Linda's behaviour shows her to be cynical and amoral. She participates actively in Irwin's scheme to rob Duddy of his hard-earned money, asking Duddy to go out on a date in order to propose the game of roulette. While on that date, she leaves Duddy, obviously in order to enjoy sexual intercourse with Peter Butler (p. 84). Most monstrous of all, however, is her association with the Boy Wonder. She is seen with him on a number of occasions in the novel and provides him with the information about Duddy's land that leads to the dramatic confrontation between Duddy and Dingleman in the last chapter.

Linda is hardly an important character in the novel, but her presence, like that of Irwin, helps to emphasize the extent of Duddy's isolation. The *pusherke* is often the object of ridicule and roguery.

Peter John Friar

Of all the small, cameo portraits in the novel, that of Peter John Friar, the pompous, untalented filmmaker, is one of the most vigorous.

Duddy first encounters Friar at Wellington College, where "the distinguished director of documentary films" is giving a lecture. Friar is vain and pompous:

> . . . He seemed especially fond of stroking his greying Van Dyke beard, knitting his fierce eyebrows, and – squinting against the smoke of a cigarette burnt perilously close to his lips – nodding as he said, 'Mm. Mm-hmm.'
>
> (p. 113)

Obviously a failure at his work, he is vague about his accomplishments. He had directed a prize-winning documentary for an oil company in Venezuela, but "for a dark reason he only hinted at" his name was not on the picture. He had left Hollywood for equally obscure reasons, murmuring mysteriously about some kind of witch-hunt. He had come to Canada from Mexico to work for the National Film Board, but according to him "he was having trouble again because he was a left-winger. " Whatever the reason, when Duddy meets him he is unemployed.

Two incidents reveal comically the pompous poseur in Friar. The first, which is his first meeting with Duddy in the bar (pp. 114ff), provides one of the funniest set pieces of comic writing in the novel. The second occasion is provided by an actual example of Friar's work — the film of the Cohen bar-mitzvah (pp. 152ff) – complete with florid commentary and unusual camera shots. These scenes are well worth close examination by the student for all that they reveal of Richler's masterful writing of comic narrative.

However, Friar is not completely devoid of ability or perceptiveness. His work is dismissed as "Amateur night in Dixie" by a professional (p. 199), but by prodigous effort he does rescue something from the disaster of the Seigel film (pp. 201ff., p. 221). Moreover, he is shrewd enough to understand exactly what Duddy is (p. 163).

Yet he is, in the end, only one of the more comic figures in the frantic career of Duddy Kravitz. Inept in his work and drunken in his habits, he eventually disappears, departing with Duddy's cameras (p. 231).

Samuel Cohen

Mr. Cohen, a metal merchant, is the epitome of the succesful Jewish business man. His credo is clearly enunciated:

. . . 'My attitude even to my oldest and dearest customer is this,' he said, making a throat-cutting gesture. If I thought he'd be good for half a cent more a ton I'd squeeze it out of him. A plague on all the *goyim,* that's my motto. The more money I make the better I take care of my own, the more I'm able to contribute to our hospital, the building of Israel, and other worthy causes.'

(pp. 265-266)

Money is Mr. Cohen's concern and his weapon against the gentiles, whom he reviles with chauvinistic bitterness.

He is both shrewd and ruthless in the pursuit of his goals. Only pressure from his family leads him to make the final deal for the bar mitzvah, but even then he bargains fiercely (pp. 149–151). Though he is furious with Duddy when the film is a commercial failure, he is nevertheless quite prepared to make a deal with him to buy Mr. Calder's scrap metal (p. 202). Further, his rise to prosperity has been fostered by criminal neglect and bribery (pp. 264ff). The only occasion on which he appears to reveal kindness occurs when he is drunk. However, that mood soon changes when he is sober and Duddy asks for help (p. 289).

The portrait of Cohen is little more than the parody of a Shylock figure, yet it has interesting aspects. For example, there is a strong suggestion that Cohen is the kind of man that Duddy will become. Cohen sees this in Duddy, for he tells the boy, "We're two of a kind" (p. 265). Therefore, his advice to Duddy (p. 266) is radically different from that offered by Uncle Benjy. Cohen may not be happy as he wanders around his fifty-thousand-dollar house (p. 267,) but he does not intend to change. In the second place, Cohen serves as the contrasting counterpart for Mr. Calder. Cohen represents the Jewish business world of Montreal, grasping, uncertain and bitter. Calder represents the Anglo-Saxon business world of Montreal, confident of its inherited wealth, more calmly shrewd and grasping, and — above all — assured.

Jerry Dingleman

Jerry Dingleman, known as the Boy Wonder since Mel West's column about him, is the folk hero of Duddy Kravitz's world. His flamboyant wealth feeds the dreams of many admirers.

Max's stories of the Boy Wonder's rise from obscurity (pp. 23ff) can hardly be received as truth, given the taxi driver's penchant for dramatic exaggeration. However, Dingleman did begin as a poor

St. Urbain Street boy. He attended Fletcher's Field High School, where he showed his gift for deception in the affair involving Mr. MacPherson's merit cards (p. 8). His family obviously contributed to his criminal leanings, for his father had been to prison and his Uncle Joe had been shot down in the days of gangster warfare. His eventual material success cannot be disputed. He owns a gambling establishment, restaurants, night clubs, and is a trafficker in drugs. Further, according to Max, he has eight racehorses running in Baltimore.

Dingleman is a cripple. At the age of twenty-eight, he had been struck by polio and now can walk only with the aid of two canes. The resulting physical changes wrought in him seem to mirror the monstrous moral character of the man:

> . . . At thirty he was no longer a handsome man. His shoulders and chest developed enormously and his legs dwindled to thin bony sticks. He put on lots of weight. Everywhere he went the Boy Wonder huffed and puffed and had to wipe the sweat from the back of his rolled hairy neck with a handkerchief. The bony head suddenly seemed massive. The grey inquisitor's eyes, whether hidden behind dark glasses – an affectation he abhorred – or flashing under rimless ones, unfailingly led people to look over his shoulder or down at the floor. His curly black hair had dried. The mouth began to turn down sharply at the corners. But the most noticeable and unexplained change was in the flesh of his face. After his illness it turned red and wet and shiny. His teeth, however, remained as white as ever and his smile was still unnervingly fresh.

(pp. 132-133)

Of course, the immediate effect of Dingleman's illness was to cause him the loss of his fiancée, Olive Brucker, whose father despatched her to Europe. She loved Dingleman, but had apparently submitted to her father's wishes. However, Dingleman's subsequent treatment of her indicates the extent of his moral depravity. She had gone through three husbands, but — more important — she "usually looked potted and there were some who said you don't get like that on booze: it was something else" (p. 133). That "something else" is undoubtedly heroin, Dingleman's chief stock-in-trade. The extent of her misery and the enormity of Dingleman's cynical depravity is seen in New York, where he is continually beseiged by a desperate woman seeking more drugs, a woman who would seem to be Olive.

Thus, for all of Max's stories of Dingleman's philanthropy, it is evident that the Boy Wonder has no regard for other people. He certainly shows no compunction in exploiting Duddy's innocence on the drug-trafficking trip to New York, and his treatment of supplicants on Schnorrer's Day hardly gives the picture of a magnanimous man.

It is to Duddy's credit that he refuses finally to enter into partnership with Dingleman, even though the grounds for refusal are personal rather than moral. An alliance with Dingleman would indeed have been a final commitment by Duddy to a way of life that is totally reprehensible. At least in the ending Duddy's naiveté still has suggestions of ambiguity, so that the reader is left with the hope that the hero may find the identity he needs.

Hugh Thomas Calder

Mr. Calder, the representative of the Anglo-Saxon business world, is a man of inherited wealth. This characteristic, of course, contrasts sharply with the Jewish businessmen in the novel — Cohen, Dingleman and Duddy — who are self-made men betraying all of the anxiety and restlessness of their kind. In contrast, Mr. Calder administers his family fortune "with conservative good sense," so that "steadily, unobtrusively he made money with his father's money" (p. 193).

Again, however, he presents us with another example of a character to whom money has not brought happiness. Like Uncle Benjy, he was usually bored. He did not enjoy his relationships with others: he was grateful for being a widower, and regarded his daughter as no more than a "true rich bitch" (p. 193). As a result, he devoted himself to short-lived and eccentric enthusiasms, the most startling of which is his habit of dropping money in toilets in order to relish the delight of speculating on who would fish it out.

Nevertheless, he is undoubtedly shrewd:

> Hugh Thomas Calder disliked Dr. Westcott intensely. He knew Sandra was not suffering from a mere nervous upset and that Westcott knew more than he was saying and – what's more – was aching to be asked about it. Calder was going to deny him that pleasure. Sandra was, to his mind, a shallow little bitch and unless it was absolutely necessary for him to know he'd much rather not get involved in what was bound to be sordid.
>
> (p. 194)

In addition, he is shrewd enough to discern Duddy's worth in the attempt to work out a solution to Lennie's problem (p. 197). Thus, Duddy's pleas for compassion for Lennie and his family receive little sympathy (p. 196), but in actual fact Duddy's persistence and courage really win the day. Duddy's forthrightness and naive aggressiveness are the qualities which gain victory and which make Calder desirous of seeing the boy again.

Calder's secure financial position and his assured social position do, of course, make him aloof and disdainful of the greed of others. That is why he is so offended by Duddy's passion for making deals. Ultimately, then, he can be of little assistance to Duddy in the furtherance of his ambitions, because he is all that Duddy is not. Confident, assured and secure, he has no wish to enter into the agonies of others.

Minor Characters

Bradley (p. 14) is Duddy's fictitious brother. He is a mere invention by Duddy, and his fabulous career — being a war hero and a movie star, and achieving great wealth — is the expression of all that Duddy would like to be.

Herbert and Clara Shields are friends of Mr. MacPherson (p. 18–19). Herbert was a fellow student at McGill and has achieved the material success that MacPherson did not. As assistant to the vice president of a pulp and paper firm, Herbert Shields, who has changed his name from the Jewish Shieldberg, is an uncomfortable reminder to MacPherson of his failure in the world. The party given by the Shields causes Mr. MacPherson to return home late, with the result that Jenny receives the fatal phone call from Duddy.

Mr. Cox is a teacher at Fletcher's Field High School and is presented as rather foolishly progressive. Like MacPherson, he does not believe in corporal punishment (p. 30). He also holds musical evenings for students at his home. There, he and his wife, Jane, try awkwardly to get to know the students better. The extent of Cox's success can be best judged by Duddy's description of Cox as "the World's No. 1 Crap-Artist" (p. 21).

Josette is a prostitute whose main claim to distinction seems to be the size of her breasts (p. 27). Max acts as her pimp.

Leonard Bush is the principal of Fletcher's Field High School. Capable and soft-spoken, he appears only briefly in the novel as "a man with many troubles." (p. 37).

Ida is the wife of Benjy Kravitz. A pants-presser's daughter, her marriage had at first been idyllic (p. 47). However, things changed when it was found that she could not bear children. In spite of her superficial, psychological explanation for what had gone wrong (pp. 236–237), it would appear that, in spite of Benjy's undiminished love for her, her reaction to her barrenness has been to turn to drink and other men. After Benjy's death, Duddy discovers her living at a hotel in Nice with a gigolo (p. 290).

Milty Halpirin is the spoiled, only child of a real estate agent (p. 49). He yearns to join Duddy's gang, the Warriors, but Duddy delights in tormenting him. The unfortunate Milty is tricked into destroying his mother's prize tulips (p. 51).

Benny Feinberg is the comical officer of the Canadian Provost Corps in charge of Duddy's neighbourhood. He takes his duties seriously — too seriously, perhaps — and Duddy deflates him completely by setting St. Urbain Street ablaze with light (pp. 52ff).

Captain John Tate is the main speaker at the Fletcher's Field Commencement (pp. 56–66). The proud descendant of a family of United Empire Loyalists, his address to the assembly is shallow and irrelevant. He is perhaps the measure of the irrelevance of the Anglo-Saxon culture to the Jewish neighbourhood.

Bernie Altaman is one of the students working at Rubin's hotel. He shows Duddy some kindness and apparently forces Irwin to return the money Duddy lost in the roulette games (p. 93).

Cuckoo Kaplan is the comedian who works at Rubin's hotel. Cuckoo was "billed as Montreal's Own Danny Kaye," but his actual talent is dubious. Each year he visited New York agents, but only had engagements in Buffalo and New Jersey. Even his father despised Cuckoo's antics:

> Cuckoo's father couldn't understand him. 'What is it with you, Chaim? For a lousy ninety dollars a week,' he said, 'to make a fool of yourself in front of all those strangers.'
>
> (p. 72)

It is predictable that Cuckoo should become the victim of Irwin, when he tricks the comedian into being left with a large bar bill (p. 72). However, Duddy and Cuckoo, neither of them popular with other people, become friends. The friendship ends abruptly when Duddy, distraught and indifferent to the feelings of friends and acquaintances, tells the comedian that he is devoid of talent (p. 253).

Shub is Jerry Dingleman's bodyguard (p. 134). A former welterweight boxer, his career had apparently been destroyed by his connection with gamblers. He is somewhat punch-drunk, and was hired by Dingleman after failing in the running of a tailor shop.

Virgil Roseboro is a young American whom Duddy meets in New York (p. 143). He sells Duddy pinball machines, which are brought over the border illegally (p. 205). He figures frequently in the narrative and would emerge as a major character, except that he is one of the less convincing figures. He is simply one of Duddy's passive victims. Duddy cheats him out of the money for the machines (pp. 215–220), and robs him of the money in his bank account (p. 304). The fact that he is an epileptic who suffers a paralyzing accident lends horror to Duddy's actions. In actual fact, in a sense Richler also exploits this character, when chapter six of part three is devoted to an example of Virgil's magazine for epileptics. In that instance the satire seems to be a rather misjudged, unworthy endeavour.

However, Duddy's exploitation of Virgil establishes firmly the parallel with Mr. Cohen, whose early attempt to make money had resulted in the death of one of his workmen.

SETTING

The immediate physical setting of *The Apprenticeship of Duddy Kravitz* is the grimy, seedy, decaying neighbourhood where Duddy lives. To a middle-class stranger, we are told, it would have looked "squalid" (p. 13). Its appearance was dominated by rickety stair-cases, peeling balconies and waste lots. Only occasionally was there a patch of well-tended grass to testify to the energy of human inhabi-tants. The aridity of this neighbourhood is confirmed by Simcha's desperate but unsuccessful attempts to make the soil yield life:

> . . . His family lived upstairs, and outside in the gritty hostile soil of his back yard, Simcha planted corn and radishes, peas, carrots, and cucumbers. Each year the corn came up scrawnier and the cucumbers yellowed before they ripened, but Simcha persisted with his planting.
>
> (p. 45)

The neighbourhood does not, of course, lack life and vitality. Duddy and his comrades relished its life. They knew and understood the varieties to be found in their environment, which was made up not only of physical factors but also of mythological lore:

> . . . No two cold-water flats were alike. Here was the house where the fabulous Jerry Dingleman was born. A few doors away lived Duddy Ash, who ran for alderman each election on a one-plank platform: provincial speedcops were anti-semites. No two stores were the same, either. Best Fruit gypped on the scales, but Smiley's didn't give credit.
>
> (p. 14)

Moreover, the rather squalid and seemingly sterile environment is the scene for very lively activities which testify to the vigour of the inhabitants. Thus, for example, the march of the Fletcher's cadets (p. 40ff), though comical and absurd, is full of the colour and action which illustrate the liveliness of the people:

> Lance-corporal Boxenbaum led with a bang bang bang on his big white drum and Litvak tripped Cohen, Pinsky blew on his bugle, and the Fletcher's Cadets wheeled left, reet, left, reet, out of Fletcher's Field, led by their Commander-in-chief, that snappy five-footer, W. E. James (that's 'Jew' spelt backwards, as he told each new gym class). Left, reet, left, reet, powdery snow crunching underfoot, Ginsburg out of step once more and Hornstein unable to beat his drum right because of the ten-on-each Mr. Caldwell had applied before the

parade. Turning smartly right down Esplanade Avenue they were at once joined and embarrassed on either side by a following of younger brothers on sleighs, little sisters with running noses, and grinning delivery boys stopping to make snowballs.

'Hey, look out there General Montgomery, here comes your mother to blow your nose.'

'Lefty! Hey, Lefty! Maw says you gotta come right home to sift the ashes after the parade. No playing pool she says. She's afraid the pipes will burst.'

Tara-boom, tara-*boom,* tara-BOOM-BOOM-BOOM, past the Jewish Old People's Home where on the balcony above, bedecked with shawls and rugs, a stain of yellowing expressionless faces, women with little beards and men with sucked-in mouths, fussy nurses with thick legs and grandfathers whose sons had little time, a shrunken little woman who had survived a pogrom and two husbands and three strokes, and two followers of Rabbi Brott the Miracle Maker, watched squinting against the fierce wintry sun.

'Jewish children in uniform?'

'Why not?'

'It's not nice. For a Jewish boy a uniform is not so nice.'

Skinny, lumpy-faced Boxenbaum took it out on the big white drum and Sergeant Grepsy Segal, who could burp or break wind at will, sang,

BULLSHIT, that's all the band could play,
BULLSHIT, it makes the grass grow green.

(pp. 40—41)

There are, in fact, many scenes which reveal vividly the irreverent, disputatious, lively nature of the neighbourhood citizens: Max's stories of the Boy Wonder (pp. 24ff); the episode involving the unfortunate Benny Feinberg (pp. 52ff); the commencement (pp. 63ff); Mr. Cohen and his family (p. 148ff).

However, it is noteworthy that even the comic description of the march of the Fletcher's Field cadets emphasizes the old people at the Jewish home. This detail introduces again the theme of decay. The activity may be lively, but it is acted out against a background of decay. This decay is an important element, which does not simply apply to the physical environment; it is an important element in the lives of the people. Thus the physical setting is only the appropriate context for what is happening to the people.

To begin with, the traditional Jewish element in their experience is waning. Benjy is a good example of what is happening. As a child, Benjy had accompanied his father regularly to the synagogue, but later Benjy "began to read Mencken and Dreiser and no longer came to pray" (p. 47). Max, with his superficial talk of *goys* and *shiksas,* is hardly a better example of religious vitality, and his pimping for

Josette does not portray moral integrity of the kind we see in Simcha. In addition, we may note that Duddy's cynical exploitation of the solemn bar mitzvah scarcely bespeaks reverence for religious tradition. In fact, the entire episode involving the bar mitzvah, for all its humour, is a revelation of the deterioration of religious tradition:

> The Cohen boy's bar mitzvah was a big affair in a modern synagogue. The synagogue in fact was so modern that it was not called a synagogue any more. It was called a Temple. Duddy had never seen anything like it in his life. There was a choir and an organ and a parking lot next door. The men not only did not wear hats but they sat together with the women. All these things were forbidden by traditional Jewish law, but those who attended the Temple were so-called reform Jews and they had modernized the law to suit life in America. The Temple prayer services were conducted in English by Rabbi Harvey Goldstone, M.A., and Cantor 'Sonny' Brown. Aside from his weekly sermon, the marriage clinic, the Sunday School, and so on, the Rabbi, a most energetic man, was very active in the community at large. He was a fervent supporter of Jewish and Gentile Brotherhood, and a man who unfailingly offered his time to radio stations as a spokesman for the Jewish point of view on subjects that ranged from 'Does Israel Mean Divided Loyalties?' to 'The Jewish Attitude to Household Pets'. He also wrote articles for magazines and a weekly column of religious comfort for the *Tely*. There was a big demand for Rabbi Goldstone as a public speaker and he always made sure to send copies of his speeches to all the newspapers and radio stations.

(p. 145)

As we read this delightful, satirical portrait of a synagogue gone modern, we can understand better the elder Mr. Cohen's tears on having to enter the building! It is best summed up perhaps by Benjy's words: ". . . this cream-puff of a synagogue, this religious drugstore, you might as well spend your life being against the *Reader's Digest*" (p. 146). In passing it is worth noting that even the criminal Dingleman finds the temple abhorrent: "I felt like a Jesuit in a whorehouse" (p. 145). The temple, then, is a graphic indication of the deterioration of the Jewish religious tradition.

Thus, it is difficult to find any committed Jews in the novel of the rank of Simcha, whose Jewishness means something to him socially, racially and morally. The others react differently to their Jewishness, but none seems to find in it spiritual strength. Max simply regrets sentimentally and unconvincingly that he has not brought his boys up to be more religious. Benjy, on the other hand, opposes his religion. Lennie is flattered that gentiles overlook his Jewishness, but after being rebuffed becomes a seemingly militant Zionist. Dingleman observes the sabbath scrupulously, but on the other days of the week is involved in the inhuman drug trade. Mr. Cohen is on the temple executive, but his dealings with Duddy reveal little compassion, and his early enterprises have been of a dubious quality, to say the least.

A number of things, of course, have obviously conspired to produce this situation. First and probably foremost, one must bear in mind the prosperous, materialstic nature of the society outside the St. Germain Street neighbourhood. Outside lie the greater comforts of Outremont and the heady luxury of Westmount. The former is attainable for some of the more prosperous Jews. The latter is another world, even though it is part of the same city, as Duddy's wonderment reveals:

> Westmount was where the truly rich lived in stone mansions driven like stakes into the shoulder of the mountain. The higher you climbed up splendid tree-lined streets the thicker the ivy, the more massive the mansion, and the more important the men inside. Mr. Calder's place was almost at the top. 'Jeez,' Duddy said aloud, getting out of his car. He had been in Westmount before in the taxi but usually at night and never this high up. Below, the city and the river hummed obligingly under a still cloud of factory fumes. What a site for a restaurant, Duddy thought. Looking up at the Calder house again he wondered what the bastard did with all those rooms.

(p. 170)

As far as the Jews of St. Urbain Street are concerned, Montreal is indeed a city divided. But it is not a city divided between the French-Canadian and the English-Canadian. It is divided between the Jews, who are poor, and the gentiles, who are not poor. To bridge the gap, it appears that the only path is that of material success. Those who do not have money, therefore, live on the accomplishments of others, like Max and his audience who revere the Boy Wonder. Those who have the initiative launch into the pursuit of money amorally, like Mr. Cohen. Duddy is the supreme example of the dreamer who eventually pursues his goal of success single-mindedly. But their object is one and the same — money.

Thus, any consideration of the setting of *The Apprenticeship of Duddy Kravitz* has to be undertaken carefully. That consideration must include an understanding of the fact that the decaying setting symbolizes, to some extent, decaying ideals. The vacuum created by the decaying ideals, together with the pressure exerted by the materialistic outside world, is filled by the desire to escape. The means of escape is seen to be material success. In that endeavour lies the vitality and the tragedy of Duddy Kravitz.

Structure

To make any reasonable critical judgements concerning the structure of *The Apprenticeship of Duddy Kravitz,* it is necessary to try to see the narrative as a whole. Structure, of course, implies the shaping of the narrative, the patient piecing-together of its elements, the flow and tempo of the events, which is directed towards achieving the dominant impression, or cluster of impressions, that the author wants to leave with the reader. In order to make clear and coherent statements about structure, then, it is, as we have stated, essential to see the novel in its entirety.

To this end, it is helpful to summarize briefly the main ingredients of the narrative, as follows:

Part One
  1. Duddy's conflicts with Mac
  2. the Cox party
  3. Max, in Eddy's Cigar & Soda
  4. Duddy's phone call to Mrs. MacPherson
  5. the march of the Fletcher's cadets
  6. Simcha and his family
  7. Duddy as a child
  8. Benjy and his family
  9. the commencement
  10. the summer at Ste Agathe

Part Two
  1. Duddy's desire to meet the Boy Wonder
  2. the meeting with Friar
  3. Cohen and the film
  4. first deposit on land
  5. Duddy, Max and Lennie
  6. interview with Dingleman
  7. trip to New York
  8. the Cohen film
  9. land purchase
  10. the search for Lennie
  11. meeting with Calder
  12. Seigal film
  13. arrival of Virgil
  14. hiring of Virgil
  15. land purchase

Part Three
1. prosperity/bohemianism
2. departure of Friar
3. Benjy's illness
4. talk with Benjy
3. Virgil's accident
6. nervous breakdown/bankruptcy
7. interlude in Ste Agathe
8. Dingleman's misfortune

Part Four
1. the frantic search for money
2. the cheating of Virgil by Duddy
3. the break with Yvette and Virgil
4. the visit to the land
5. the confrontation with Dingleman
6. the disappointment of Simcha
7. Max and Duddy in the bar

Even cursory perusal of the elements of the plot in this fashion reveals an unmistakable characteristic of the narrative; namely, that it is not unusual or experimental in form. The story is told generally in chronological order. Part one does have sections which are an exception to this conclusion. There, the story opens with Duddy as a fifteen-year-old and then goes back in time to earlier episodes in his life. However, even there the switch in time is only temporary. Once the childhood of the character has been sketched in and the context of his family has been depicted, the chronological treatment resumes and continues to the end of the novel. Thus, the four sections form part of a logical, coherent pattern, each part of which might be given a caption, thus:

Part One: The Character of the Hero and the Nature of his Dream
Part Two: The Struggle to Achieve the Dream
Part Three: Crisis
Part Four: The Achievement of the Dream.

This orthodoxy of form is consonant with the focus of the novel, which is intentionally directed sharply upon the central character, Duddy Kravitz. The vividly realized characterization of Duddy is the largest contributor to the structural unity of the book. His personality — ambitious, anxious, gauche, inventive, egocentric and yet at times pitifully seeking human warmth — is the personality that dominates It is a shrewdly created presence. Duddy might easily have alienated any reader. His insensitive aggressiveness and his single-minded passion for recognition border on the monstrous. Neither at the beginning nor at the end is he an admirable person. He is assuredly not a hero one might wish to emulate. Even at the end, his naive rejoicing in his seeming victory hardly stirs the response of exultation in the reader. Yet we cannot view him as a monster. His recognizable human qualities temper harsh criticism and disarm violent condemnation. In this reaction, perhaps it is the wistful quality associated with Duddy that overcomes our rejection. Because of his poor social position, because of his aching need for affection and esteem from his own family, because of the naiveté with which he pursues his goal, he becomes recognizable to us as, in a sense, all alienated men in modern society. We understand the need for his dream and, however uncomfortably, the passion with which the dream is pursued. The novel, then, is not simply about the modern conflict between materialism and human fulfilment, but also about the "lostness' of man and his desire to know his place in the world. It is fitting, therefore, that Duddy and his dream should be at the heart of the novel and provide its unity. As a result, the form of the novel becomes, as many have observed, picaresque in quality. Duddy is the innocent who goes out to pit himself against the world. His tilting with the world is the central concern. The other characters and all of the situations revolve around that.

To underline this central concern, the novel is unified by a motif which runs through its pages. The motif is provided by Simcha, who tells his seven-year-old grandson: "A man without land is nothing." Duddy never forgets these words. They become his statement of faith, his motto in his battle with the world. He never questions the meaning of the words, and he never doubts their validity. If he had, he might have reached Dingleman's insight and seen that they were simply the expression of human yearning, not intended to be fulfilled and perhaps not even desired in reality. However, Duddy took the advice literally, and on a number of occasions justifies his actions by using them. In the end, the emptiness of his grandfather's words is evident, and Duddy is left mouthing them pitiably (p. 313).

Simcha's words to Duddy compromise only one of the trite sayings in the novel, which is liberally sprinkled with platitudes. "Anatomy's the killer," declares Lennie sententiously. His words mean very little. They are simply the sounds he uses to evade harsh reality, the harsh reality of the complex, difficult tasks facing him in his studies and the harsh reality of his folly and neglect. The words are an absurd simplification of complex human experience. Significantly, both Max and

Duddy seize upon them and echo them. Thus, together with the other platitudes in the novel — "When I lose my temper, I lose my temper"; "Man does not live by bread alone"; "Money is the root of all evil" — they form a chorus of sounds testifying to shallow thinking and superficial attitudes. In this way, they all compose a motif which comments upon the central concern of the novel and helps to bring it unity.

The structure of *The Apprenticeship of Duddy Kravitz* displays, then, careful architecture, in which character, theme and motifs combine to form that pleasing unity which is part of the novel's effectiveness. The careful shaping of the narrative is abundantly evident upon a closer examination of part three. This section of the work is reminiscent of the effect often achieved in the third act of a Shakespearean tragedy, for it reveals the hero at a critical stage of his career. Duddy is enjoying prosperity of a kind hitherto unknown to him. His bohemianism is a sign both of that prosperity and of his inability to cope with the new experience. However, two crucial events take place which have a bearing on Duddy's destiny. The first is Benjy's illness, which leads to the confrontation between uncle and nephew. That confrontation reveals clearly the choice which is open to Duddy. He can continue as he is doing and become a successful "Jew-boy on the make," or he can refashion his life in order to become the man Simcha had seen in him. Duddy, aware of the choice, flees from the truth revealed in the confrontation. It is then that the second event takes place. Virgil has the terrible accident with the truck. Disaster follows quickly, with Duddy's nervous breakdown and his bankruptcy.. It would seem at this point that it is now more possible for Duddy to fulfil his grandfather's hopes for himself and to reject the path towards which materialism and acquisitiveness had been pushing him. As a sign of this, the narrative shows the interlude at Ste Agathe, when Duddy is reunited with Virgil and Yvette, two of the "good" characters in the novel. However, part three closes with an event which reveals definitively the real bent of Duddy's character — the exposure of Dingleman's drug trafficking. Duddy's response to this revelation shows the young man's dedication to the ambition which once already had brought prosperity. Thus, the denouement flows inexorably from the crisis.

The narrative does not, however, always display such singleness of purpose on the part of the author. One could, for example, complain that at times Richler's fondness for staging comic scenes overcomes his desire for total structural unity. Thus, the account of the march of the Fletcher's cadets, while without doubt an admirable example of comic writing, is hardly justified in terms of the novel as a whole. Some of the earlier scenes involving Mr. Mac-Pherson and the chapter devoted entirely to the reproduction of an issue of Virgil's magazine for epileptics might be regarded as falling into the same category.

Nevertheless, *Duddy Kravitz* displays an admirable concern for form, which does contribute to the effectiveness of the novel. It is testimony to Richler's artistry that he has given the novel such careful structure without sacrificing the sense of vitality we appreciate in the multitude of characters, impressions and events which is *The Apprenticeship of Duddy Kravitz*.

PURPOSE AND THEME

In *The Uncertain World,* Mordecai Richler, discussing his reasons for being a writer, reaffirms a statement by George Orwell and adds an important qualification to it:

"4. Political purpose — using the word 'political' in the widest possible sense. Desire to push the world in a certain direction, to alter other people's ideas of the kind of society that they should strive after." Not an overlarge consideration in my work, though I would say that any serious writer is a moralist, and only incidentally an entertainer.

The statement has relevance to *The Apprenticeship of Duddy Kravitz.* It acts as a warning, in the first place, that it would be naive of the reader to judge the book as simply a comic novel. Richler is not merely acting the part of the novelist as entertainer in the work. The temptation to adopt this view is obvious, for many of the comic moments are in fact immensely entertaining. There are indeed a number of scenes which are enjoyable for their buffoonery. The march of the Fletcher's cadets, the account of Cuckoo Kaplan and, to a lesser extent, the scenario for the Cohen bar mitzvah – all are examples of "set" scenes in which comic pleasure seems to be the main element and intention. However, there is much evidence of another kind of humour, in which the laughter is mixed with other elements, so that the total effect which is achieved is much more complex than that of simple enjoyment of the comedy. A minor example of this might be Duddy's interview with Sandra Calder:

Ten minutes passed. Sandra lit a cigarette. 'I'm not going to talk to you any more,' she said. 'I'm going to ignore you.'

'Don't make *me* cry,' Duddy said.

'I'm going up to my room.'

There was a pause. 'Well,' Duddy asked, 'what's keeping you?'

'Aren't you going?'

'I'm waiting here for your father. I told you that.'

'If I gave you his address would you promise not to make any trouble?'

'Give me his address. Come on.'

Sandra wrote out the address and led him through the dining-room again.

"You could fit a bowling alley into here. Jeez.'

'I don't even know your name. All you told me is that you're his brother.'

'Dudley: I'm in the film business. An indie.'

'I beg your pardon?'

'An independent producer,' he said, handing her his card. 'Hey, you must know a lot of debutantes like . . . '

Sandra was still absorbed by his card.

'Listen,' Duddy said, 'have you ever heard of John Peter Friar?' He told her about him. 'We could do a top-notch picture on a coming-out party. A record for your grandkiddies and their grandkiddies after them.'

Sandra smiled.

'Don't lose that card. You get us a job in Westmount and there'll be something in it for you. I'm no piker, you know.'

'Do I look as if I need the money?'

'I never met a pretty girl who couldn't use a few extra bucks for a nice dress.'

'Tell Leonard not to worry.'

'Can do,' Duddy said. 'Cheerio '

(p. 179)

The scene is over in a moment, but its humour is obvious. However, the laughter is not simply extraneous comedy. It is an effective vehicle for reinforcing our grasp of Duddy's naiveté. Thus the humour springs directly from the characterization; it is part of the incongruity inherent in Duddy. On the one hand, he is a person of enormous aspirations. He takes himself very seriously; he is an "indie." On the other hand, he is often absurdly naive, as when he soberly assures Sandra of "a few extra bucks for a nice dress." Hence, the total effect is more complex than that gained by comic farce. It has elements of pathos which are an inescapable part of the human condition, for the contrast between man's aspirations and man's accomplishments, between what he aspires to be and what he shows himself to be, is an inherent aspect of the divine animal we call man. The gap between aspiration and performance is thus a fruitful source of tragedy, of comedy and of tragi-comedy, depending upon what view of the human condition the writer adopts. Much of the humour in *The Apprenticeship of Duddy Kravitz* springs from the writer's apprehension of this "gap". The reader can, no doubt, find many examples:

1. most of the scenes involving the unfortunate Mr. MacPherson
2. Duddy's interview with Mr. Cohen (pp. 122ff)
3. Duddy's encounter with the Boy Wonder (pp. 131ff)
4. Duddy's attempt to borrow money from his father (pp. 292ff)
5. Duddy's treatment of Dingleman (p. 311)
6. Duddy's moment of triumph (p. 316).

The humour in the novel, then, is not simply an entertaining extra, a kind of sugar coating laid upon the more bitter pill of Richler's theme. Much of the humour is an intrinsic illustration of Richler's view of the human condition, for it is rooted in the basic incongruity that is man.

A further aspect of the quotation from *The Uncertain World* is Richler's assertion of political purpose. That does not mean, of course, purpose as exercised in politics, but purpose directed towards man's way of ordering his existence. It is the kind of purpose born in the writer's apprehension of what is wrong in society and in his desire to "push the world in a certain direction."

On the simplest, most basic level, this underlines the satirical element of the novel. Certainly, Richler is a merciless satirist of the society of men. His targets are many and varied in *Duddy Kravitz*. For example, one target is that favoured by all satirists — human hypocrisy. The pseudo-intellectuals are vivid examples of this kind of attack. Thus, one of Duddy's bohemian acquaintances, Blum the poet, is exposed mercilessly:

> . . . The hardest to get rid of, however, was the fierce editor of *Attack!* Blum never left until the last bottle was empty. Virgil adored him. After the others had gone he would sit on the floor and Blum would recite his latest poems to him in a booming voice. 'I can't understand it,' Blum said, 'when you think how well-known the other poets of my generation are . . . Spender and Dylan and George Barker . . . I can't understand it . . .'
> When he had too much to drink and began to cry Blum reminded Duddy of Cuckoo Kaplan. Hersh didn't like Blum. 'An unsigned copy of his poems,' he said, 'is a collector's item.'

(pp. 224–225)

On a similarly comic level is the satiric portrait of Rabbi Goldstone, which displays with knife-like precision the pompous aridity of the religious leader, "who unfailingly offered his time to radio stations as a spokesman for the Jewish point of view on subjects that ranged from 'Does Israel Mean Divided Loyalties?' to 'The Jewish Attitude to Household Pets.'" It is little wonder that the elder Cohen was reluctant to enter the rabbi's synagogue, being firmly convinced that it was actually a church! Sometimes, of course, the satire has darker tones to it, as with the treatment Richler gives to Cohen. Thus, Cohen may seem to be at first simply the comic stereotype of the Jewish businessman, but later his hypocritical rapaciousness is revealed as being criminal and inhuman. Hypocrisy, however, is not the only target. Richler is also a critic of society's worship of materialism. Thus Dingleman has his fervent disciples, even though his wealth, which is what brings him the veneration, is based upon actvities that contribute to human misery. Further, that Duddy's eventual triumph is founded upon the wreckage of human values, such as loyalty and compassion and honesty, is a vivid condemnation of the god of materialism that society worships. In the materialistic sense, Duddy does win, and society immediately accords him the victor's reward; he becomes not Duddy Kravitz, but "the Mr. Kravitz who just bought all that land round Lac St. Pierre" (p. 315). Constantly, Richler raises the targets and pierces them unerringly:

1. the educational system, as represented by Mr. MacPherson and his colleagues
2. the complacent smugness of the *nouveau-riche,* as represented by the Jews who throng Ste Agathe
3. the combination of ignorance and egotism, as represented by Max
4. the futile and insincere Zionism of Jews such as Lennie
5. the careless irresponsibility of those who are young and rich, such as Sandra Calder and her friends

This list is minimal and indicates some of the satirical targets in fairly general terms. There are, in addition, numerous small details embedded in larger scenes which reveal the satirical intention of the novel.

However, in terms of theme surely Richler's purpose is larger than the satirical. To be specific, the novel appears to offer comment upon two important aspects of human life.

In the first place, *Duddy Kravitz* voices biting condemnation of what Desmond Pacey has called "the life of materialistic acquisitiveness." This thrust of the novel is more than mere satirical comment. The theme is an integral part of the work. In a sense, Duddy's apprenticeship is, then, a kind of extended metaphor of the theme. The materialistic values of society are stressed very early in the novel. The first character to appear, Mr. MacPherson, is the embodiment of defeated idealism. He began his career with noble dreams, but harsh reality shattered the visions. In the end, it is his failure in materialistic terms which is an important ingredient in his sense of defeat. Herbert Shields is the instrument whereby MacPherson confesses the extent of his failure:

Once in the taxi he recalled how Herbert had introduced him to a group of strangers. 'I want you to shake the hand of the most brilliant student of our class at McGill. He could have been a success at anything he wanted. Instead he's devoted his life to teaching.' It was clear that they still took him for the freshly scrubbed idealist who had left McGill twenty years ago. They had no idea that he was exhausted, bitter, and drained, and that given the chance to choose again he would never become a teacher.

(p. 31)

MacPherson might dismiss the Shields as "materialists" or "philistines", but he could not help judging his life according to their terms. He knew the truth that they would report to friends — he was a failure (pp. 13–14). But evidence of materialistic values abounds. Thus, Mr. Cohen may be an officer at his synagogue, but his real credo is money:

> . . . 'My attitude even to my oldest and dearest customer is this,' he said, making a throat-cutting gesture. 'If I thought he'd be good for half a cent more a ton I'd squeeze it out of him. A plague on all the *goyim*, that's my motto. The more money I make the better I take care of my own, the more I'm able to contribute to our hospital, the building of Israel, and other worthy causes.'

(pp. 265–266)

There is no genuine religious impulse behind this affirmation. Cohen's hatred of the *goyim* is not based upon religious conviction. They are simply people unlike himself who either bar his way to money or else can be exploited in the pursuit of money. Consequently, if money is involved, religious convictions can be sacrificed. For example, Cohen is eager to do business with Calder. This underlines Richler's observation that it is not religious, racial or language differences which divide Montreal, but rather class differences. There are two camps, those who have money and those who do not have money, so that, as Richler pointed out to Nathan Cohen in an interview, "the middle-class Jew has much more in common with the middle-class Gentile than he has with the Jew who works for him in his factory." Money is the bond, and money is the supreme value. Thus Max may talk in hollow fashion of money being the root of all evil, yet it is precisely the wonder of wealth, especially wealth used flamboyantly, that is the source of his veneration of the Boy Wonder. That wealth overrides all other considerations, so that when Dingleman is revealed as a criminal Max offers no condemnation on moral grounds. He exults in the expectation that his hero will escape without penalty:

> . . . 'Boy, the Wonder's lined up the sharpest battery of legal-eagles in the country. He's playing it smart too. He's got Shubert — that's

the brains of the outfit, I figure — and two bigshot *goys* for display. Aw, they'll wipe the floor with Cote.'

(p. 292)

Even Uncle Benjy has not been deaf to the insistent materialistic urgings of society. He did succeed materially, but later he recognized the cost, and tried to warn Duddy:

> . . . I didn't like you because you're a throwback, Duddel. I'd look at you and remember my own days as a hungry salesman in the mountains and how I struggled for my first little factory. I'd look at you and see a busy, conniving little yid, and I was wrong because there was more, much more. But there's something you ought to know about me. Every year of my life I have looked back on the man I was the year before — the things I did and said — and I was ashamed. All my life I've ridiculed others, it's true, but I was the most ridiculous figure of all, wasn't I?

(pp. 278–279)

The awareness came too late for Benjy, but he wanted desperately to help save Duddy. For that reason he left Duddy no money in his will. Duddy was given only the house with the fine library, the house that could not be sold or rented. However, the warning came too late. Immediately after reading Benjy's letter, Duddy revisits his property and relives his materialistic dream:

> There could have been a real snazzy hotel and a camp, the finest ski-tow money could buy, canoes, cottages, dancing on the lake, bonfires, a movie, a skating rink, fireworks on Israeli Independence Day, a synagogue, a Western-style saloon, and people saying, 'Good morning, sir,' adding in a whisper after he'd passed, 'That was Kravitz. He built the whole shebang. They used to say he was a dreamer and he'd never make it.'

(p. 280)

The vision is absurd in its details of a hodgepodge, tasteless development built to the glorification of the fast buck. Yet Duddy is not to be totally blamed for the tawdriness of his dream. He had been simply a willing pupil under the tutelage of a grossly materialistic society. He was not deceived; the lesson had been clear and his choice unswerving. As he began his quest, he had observed shrewdly the real values of people like Linda Rubin, and he faced the challenge unwaveringly:

> Look at me, he thought, take a good look because maybe I'm dirt now. Maybe I've never been to Paris and I don't know a painter from a horse's ass. I can't play tennis like the other guys here, but I don't

go around spilling ketchup in other guy's beds either. I don't trick guys into crazy promises when they're drunk. I don't speak dirty like you either. You make fun of your father. You don't like him. Tough shit. But he sends you to Europe and Mexico and who pays for those drinks in the afternoon? You're sorry for making a fool out of me. Gee whizz, my heart bleeds. Take a good look, you dirty bitch. Maybe I'm dirt today. That bastard of a black marketeer Cohen can give me twenty bucks and a lecture about gambling and feel good for a whole week. But you listen here, kiddo. It's not always going to be like this. If you want to bet on something then bet on me. I'm going to be a somebody and that's for sure.

(p. 95)

Thus Duddy's challenge to "crap-artists" like Uncle Benjy, whose money allows them to be condescending towards those who have no money, is just: "You think I should be running after something else besides money? Good. Tell me what" (p. 242). There is no satisfactory answer for Duddy; Simcha's advice is ambiguous, and Benjy's advice is given too late.

Consequently, it is entirely consonant with society's real values that in the end Duddy should be recognized as a winner. Max creates a new myth to regale his listeners — the myth of Duddy Kravitz, who from the day of his birth was "slated for fame and fortune" (p. 315). The seal of approval is finally attached when we see that Duddy Kravitz is now Mr. Kravitz, the landowner who is worthy of credit. He reveals in his new status (p. 316). However, the final scene is full of incisive irony. Duddy is oblivious to the price that has been paid, but the reader is not. In Duddy's path, stretching behind him and marking the way he has taken, lie the regrets of Benjy, the disappointment of Simcha, the misery of Virgil, the broken heart of Yvette, and the ruins of the man that Duddy might have been. All are testimony to the havoc wrought by a materialistic society.

A second theme of the novel is that of the alienation of man in modern society. It flows, of course, from the materialistic passion of society. Where things take precedence over people, true humanness is lost. Man loses his sense of relationship with other men, who become mere instruments in the satisfaction of his desire for possessions. The consequences for society are grave, but the consequences are equally serious for the individual. For the true self is found in relationship with others. Man needs not only the "I," but also the "Thou" in order to discover and develop his human qualities.

In *The Apprenticeship of Duddy Kravtiz,* there is possibly only one human relationship — that between Virgil and Yvette. However, even that can hardly be considered as normal, in view of Virgil's paralysis. Moreover, is does seem to depend upon Yvette's self-sacrifice rather than upon any equality in the human exchange. Nevertheless, the relationship does show the possibilities which true giving and exchanging of a nonmaterialistic kind can fulfil. For example, as a result of Yvette's concern, Virgil is able to survive his misfortune and find useful employment. On the other side, Yvette, in response to Virgil's need, becomes a secretary and establishes a dignified existence for herself. In contrast, other relationships in the novel are so sterile as to suffocate truly human possibilities. Simcha, the man with spiritual potential, is a deeply disappointed man: his marriage has obviously disappointed him; Max has disappointed him; Benjy has disappointed him; and Duddy is probably the greatest disappointment of all. The disappointment has nothing to do with money; it is caused by the nature of those whom he loved. For this reason, he declares himself a failure (p. 48). Further, Max seems to be incapable of any meaningful relationships. His memories of his wife involve only such superficial things as listening to the Lux Theatre; he remembers Duddy's childhood only for the fact that the boy's illnesses had caused him the inconvenience of missing favourite radio programmes. Benjy showers attention and gifts upon Lennie, but Lennie dislikes his uncle. The marriage between Benjy and Ida is shattered. Mr. Calder is grateful for the fact that he is a widower, and he dismisses his own daughter as a "rich bitch" (p. 193). The depth of the relationship in Mr. Cohen's marriage is obviously conspicuous by its absence:

> . . . It had cost him fifty thousand dollars to build the house, his wife's dream, and the only room he could tolerate was the kitchen. Mr. Cohen got up and looked in the fridge. With his wife up north for the summer, he had a rest from that stinky new-style Chinese food, all those nuts and pineapple and not a chunk of meat anywhere as big as your toe-nail. With his wife away he was even able to keep a smoked meat in the fridge. There was nobody to lecture him about calories and stomach linings and fatty tissue around the heart. He made himself an enormous sandwich, leaned back, and let out a resounding burp.
>
> It's my house, he thought, and I can do what I want here.
>
> (p. 267)

The relationships in *Duddy Kravitz* are thus probably best summed up in Benjy's judgement of the relationships within his family: "We eat each other up . . . " (p. 242).

Lack of meaningful relationship is not the only mark of alienation. A second aspect is unhappiness which, in the novel, often
appears as boredom with life. Thus, in spite of his material success,
Benjy is bored (p. 59). Calder is so bored with his existence that
he invents petty "enthusiams" to stimulate himself, deriving particular
pleasure from observing cynically the effect which money has upon
people (pp. 193–194). With his wife gone for the summer, Mr. Cohen
is bored and hardly satisfied with his existance as he roams through
his empty house (p. 267). The problem is obvious: when the
only stimulation to which they respond – the pursuit of money –
is removed, the characters have nothing left. Thrown back upon
themselves, they look inward and find nothing. This is inevitably
to be Duddy's destiny also. His interest in cultural things has been
fleeting, mere indulgence in his momentary prosperity, and he
has rejected love in the person of Yvette. Significantly, when
financial disaster does arrive and he is left alone, he suffers a
nervous breakdown. For his pursuit of possessions has destroyed
all other dimensions of his being. Those who were most loyal to
him, Yvette and Virgil, are sacrificed on the altar of his acquisitiveness. With them vanished his opportunity for true selfhood. He
must inevitably become as hollow as the other characters in the novel.

In summary, it is obvious that *Duddy Kravitz* is more than a
satirical comedy. Richler's themes are serious and important: the
destructive nature of society's veneration of materialism, and the
consequent self-alienation of modern man. These themes do indeed
underline the serious and vigorous political purpose of the novel.

OTHER NOVELS BY MORDECAI RICHLER

A word of caution and of explanation is necessary in this section of these notes. In a volume of these dimensions, it is necessary to be selective. Thus, this section deals with three novels by Mordecai Richler. It cannot hope to be comprehensive. However, two considerations have dominated both the choice and the technique of the selection. In the first place, the three novels chosen – *Son of a Smaller Hero, The Incomparable Atuk* and *St. Urbain's Horseman* – illustrate three aspects of Richler's work as a novelist. The first, which is the second novel that he wrote, finds him exploring for the first time the Montreal ghetto which was to be the setting for *The Apprenticeship of Duddy Kravitz* and which was to furnish the metaphors that express his concern with central problems such as alienation and identity. *The Incomparable Atuk* is included because the technique and the setting are different from those of the Montreal novels. Finally, *St. Urbain's Horseman* is examined because it illustrates a more mature Richler in terms of technique and the drawing together of the artistic threads of the earlier novels. The selection, then, is purposeful, and the reader should be aware of that purpose. In the second place, the reader should recognize the limitations of the treatment offered here. The analyses which follow do not pretend to be complete or comprehensive. Many of the statements made would really demand much fuller consideration to be accepted readily as valid. Above all, the outlines are not meant to be a substitute for a careful reading of the books in question. Quotation is used liberally, not as a substitute for reading the original, but simply so that the reader may judge for himself the validity of the ideas presented and may gain a truer picture of the method of the novel being discussed.

Son of a Smaller Hero

This is Richler's second novel, and in some ways it bears the marks of the novelist's apprenticeship. The reader who has encountered *The Apprenticeship of Duddy Kravitz* and, better still, *St. Urbain's Horseman* will without doubt feel that in this early novel the author works less deftly and subtly than he does in his later work. To begin with, the handling of the material to be presented is more pedestrian than in the novels produced later. Richler speaks to the reader more directly. Rather than suggesting responses, he tells more prosaically the response which he is trying to evoke. This causes a certain unevenness in, for example, the passages which are intended to create the setting. Thus, on the one hand Richler etches in the environment with Dreiser-like flatness and dullness:

> All day long St. Lawrence Boulevard, or Main Street, is a frenzy of poor Jews, who gather there to buy groceries, furniture, clothing, and meat. Most walls are plastered with fraying election bills, in Yiddish, French, and English. The street reeks of garlic, and quarrels and bill collectors: orange crates, stuffed full with garbage and decaying fruit, are piled slipshod in most alleys. Swift children gobble pilfered plums, slower cats prowl the fish market. After the water truck has passed, the odd dead rat can be seen floating down the gutter followed fast by rotten apples, cigar butts, chunks of horse manure, and a terrifying zigzag of flies. Few stores go in for subtle window displays. Instead, their windows are jammed full and pasted with streamers that say ALL GOODS REDUCED or EVERYTHING MUST GO.

The passage is somewhat tedious. The selection of details is, at best, conventional. The tempo is flat, and it reads rather like a school exercise. Yet a different Richler is at work elsewhere. For example, he can depict the spirit of the ghetto with great vividness:

> The ghetto of Montreal has no real walls and no true dimensions. The walls are the habit of atavism and the dimensions are an illusion. But the ghetto exists all the same. The fathers say: "I work like this so it'll be better for the kids." A few of the fathers, the dissenters, do not crowd their days with work. They drink instead. But in the end it amounts to the same thing: in the end, work in textile or garment factories. Some are orthodox, others void.

A similar unevenness can be found in the presentation of the characters. Noah's reflections about Shloime illustrate the "telling" technique — Richler asks the questions that the reader should be left to ask for himself:

> Noah's attention faltered. Shloime's speech was an incongruous mixture of newspaper editorials, army lectures, and ghetto fear. Obviously, Shloime had found his level. He was a fully adjusted member. Had Melech Adler abandoned love for the sake of righteousness and come to America to produce this dangerously small man? Was this boy the end-product of religious fanaticism?

The reader can hardly escape the fact that here he is being told what attitude he ought to adopt to Shloime. "Obviously," Richler declares,

"Shloime had found his level." Obviously, the reader is being taught explicitly what to think. However, on other occasions, the technique is much more subtle. The attitude then is communicated indirectly through seemingly minor details. A response is evoked, rather than directed. For example, when Noah goes to visit Panofsky, the rather old-fashioned man with communistic leanings, one small detail suffices to call forth the response that Richler seeks:

> The room was papered yellow and three pictures hung on the walls. One of Marx; one of Lenin; and one of Mrs. Panofsky, who was also dead.

These observations are not intended to imply that the novel is of little value. That would be an unjust, hasty conclusion. The book is written with a tenderness and compassion that are haunting. Those qualities lift its appeal far above the closed walls of the Jewish ghetto and give it a far wider audience than that of the Jew who faces daily the conflict between racial tradition and individual freedom. True, the Jew's problem is at the forefront. Noah Adler feels trapped. On the one hand is the austere person of his grandfather, Melech, who has become in his community the voice of stern, orthodox religion:

> . . . The Adlers lived in a cage and that cage, with all its faults, had justice and safety and a kind of felicity. A man knew where he stood. *Melech rules.* The nature of the laws did not matter nearly as much as the fact that they had laws. (Italics added)

Thus, Melech's God was "stern, sometimes just, and always without mercy." On the other hand, there is the shadowy figure of his maternal grandfather, Jacob Goldenberg, the wise, compassionate Zaddik whose spiritual claims, voiced in the person of Leah, were equally insistent. Noah can accept neither of them as his model. He has quarrelled with Melech over the old man's immoral deception of Mr. Moore, the *goy,* and cannot accept his incredible self-righteous confidence in his Jewishness. He is alienated by his mother's romantic religious dreams which are an inheritance from her father. Thus he seeks to disentangle himself from the snares of the tradition which is his:

> "Nothing is absolute any longer, Mr. Panofsky. There is a choice of beliefs and a choice of truths to go with them. If you choose not to choose then there is no truth at all. There are only points of view . . . "
>
> "Still, that is no answer."
>
> "What if there are no answers? Or if the answers are not suitable — what then? Perhaps there are only more questions."

But the problem that the novel presents is not simply a Jewish problem. Its scope is wider. It is the problem faced by all men who live in a universe that is fundamentally a mystery to them. Their responses may differ. They may choose to defy the threat of meaninglessness with the affirmation of absolutes, or they may retreat into the solace of a mysticism that blurs the harshness of reality. The problem remains, humanly agonizing and persistently urgent. It is the problem of living an existence that is fraught with impermanence and threatened with meaninglessness. All of the characters feel the sharpness of the problem in varying degrees. Even the harsh Melech is a man poring over his dreams of what might have been. For decades he has treasured his mementoes of the Polish girl he might have married, had he been permitted. They lie stored in a tin box, along with the parchments he has clumsily inscribed — the parchments which are the evidence of his shattered dream of becoming a scribe. Leah is consumed with regret. She does not find in her husband, Wolf, any sign of the deep piety and religious compassion and sensitivity she had known in her father. She is living on the strength of dying dreams, and her illness is merely symbolic of her condition. Miriam, the *goy,* is tormented by dreams. Trapped in a lifeless marriage with Theo Hall, she is tortured by memories of her broken, disappointed and drunken father who committed suicide. Futilely, she seeks a man who will rekindle her sense of the vitality of life, who will refurbish the romantic dreams and will offer escape from harsh reality. She is not naive. At first she welcomes Noah as the answer to her yearnings, but her joy, she knows instinctively, will be short-lived. The interlude with Noah at St. Adele is an interlude and no more. When the idyll is over, she returns to her husband, becoming insolently promiscuous but pathetically more distressed. Wolf Adler is as lost as anyone in the novel. He cannot measure up to his wife's expectations of him; he cannot emulate the dead Jacob Goldenberg. He reacts negatively. He goes alone to the movies twice each Sunday, and continually tells obscene jokes. His synagogue observances are simply a desperate attempt to please his father, Melech. He seeks to achieve his identity, his sense of worth as a person, by trying to persuade his father to grant him a partnership in the coal business. He yearns continually for the money he believes his father keeps in the tin box. Ironically, he dies in the fire which destroys the office. He had sought to rescue the box from the flames, the box which contained religious scrolls and romantic mementoes. Thus he is remembered as the man who died to save the Torah. His death was given a meaning which his life would never have achieved.

The message is clear and compelling. Faced with the awesome task of living, men and women resort to facades which hide their frustrations and longings:

> . . . He finally realized that the secret of their humanity was that each one had a tiny deviation all his and/or her own. None conformed completely. Marsha, the little bitch, had love being made to her by a McGill quarterback whilst she was trying to hook Noah. (That finally endeared her to him.) His Aunt Rachel obeyed in all things except that she secretly read the most blatantly pornographic literature, and Mrs. Feldman beat her French poodle with a whip. Terror lurked behind their happiness. In fact, they weren't happy at all: they were composed. Truth was adroitly side-stepped, like a dog's excrement on the footpath. Harvey was obviously a repressed homosexual. Everybody knew, nobody agreed to see. That lie was the strength that held the Goldenbergs together.

Noah's insight into the truth is the source of the hopeful tone at the end of the novel. He has selfishly sought his answers. Thus, he exploited Theo Hall cynically; he selfishly sought the realization of a romantic dream with Miriam; he quarrelled openly with Melech; and in the end he left his mother. His decisions are prompted by considerations that frequently take into account his own longings and aspirations. However, a strong note of compassion is sounded. Before leaving for Europe, he does effect reconciliation of a kind with Melech. He responds to the shattered dreams that the old man has stored in the tin box and asks for a parchment that he can take with him to Europe. The future is still by no means certain. The sweetness of reconciliation is marred still by suggestions of the inadequacy of human compassion. Noah kisses his grandfather, but the kiss has elements of judgemnt in it:

> "After he had gone Melech touched his cheek and felt that kiss like a burn. He touched his cheek and felt that he had been punished."

The same element is clear in Melech's response. He settles back into his life, and the source of his comfort is obvious:

> Each man creates God in his own image. Melech's God, who was stern, sometimes just, and always without mercy, would reward him and punish the boy. Melech could count on that.

Nevertheless, Noah has had his vision of the human condition. He can never again be the same young man who had impatiently moved away from his family to take a room on Dorchester Street. He has seen and, perhaps most significantly, he has admitted to himself that he has seen.

Son of a Smaller Hero is an impressive accomplishment. Its scale may at first seem to be small and limited, for Richler keeps his view tightly focused on the world of the Montreal ghetto. However, the quality of the accomplishment can be seen clearly in the way in which the novelist has employed that narrow environment in such a way as to make it a microcosm of the human experience. The novel, then, is not significant simply as a Jewish novel. It is not significant simply as a Canadian novel. It is a novel which is significant on a much more universal, human level. It portrays with credibility and sensitivity an important aspect of what might be called the human condition. For it speaks compassionately not of narrow concerns – Jewishness, biculturalism, Canadian identity – but of the dreams that warm human hearts, of the disappointments that visit men and women and of the agonizing questions that torment humanity.

The Incomparable Atuk

As many critics have pointed out, Richler took for his model for this book Voltaire's *L'Ingénu,* the story of a Huron Indian transported to the sophisticated, corrupt and experienced world of Paris in the eighteenth century. Thus the immediate expectation is that of a variation on the innocence/experience theme. However, the reader's expectations are jolted immediately. The first startling item is Richler's choice of an epigraph for his novel:

> What would happen in Canada if full sovereignty were invoked and the southern border were sealed tight against American mass culture — if the air-waves were jammed, if all our comic books were embargoed, if only the purest and most uplifting of American cultural commodities were allowed entry? Native industries would take over, obviously. *Cut off from American junk, Canada would have to produce her own.* (Italics added)

Richard H. Rovere, *Macleans,* Nov. 5, 1960 The second jolt is the nature of the Eskimo hero, Atuk. He is certainly not the traditional model of the Noble Savage. He takes to the squalid mass culture of Toronto as though born into it. Once in the city, he has no intention of returning to his home:

> The success of Atuk's book was such that he was flown to Toronto for a literary party at the Park Plaza Hotel. His thoughtful publisher laid in a supply of chocolate bars and put some raw salmon on ice. A press conference was arranged. Atuk was interviewed on television. He was taken to see a midget wrestling match, a striperama, Rabbi Glen Seigal's Temple, and other wonders of Toronto. Afterwords Atuk simply refused to return to the Bay.

Further, there is no sign of primitive innocence in his successful seduction of Bette Dolan, the champion swimmer of Lake Ontario, who was so much a Canadian heroine that she had refused to give herself to any man. Atuk swiftly finds in Bette the weakness by which he can conquer her: her selfish, egotistical pride in helping others:

> So Atuk told her his dreadful secret. "I lack confidence," he said, "because I am unable to make love. All that stands between me and hitting the bull's eye is a woman who can . . . well, encourage me over the hump." He lowered his head. "I need help, Miss Dolan."
>
> A plea for help was something Bette Dolan had never taken lightly. She sprang to her feet, bouncing upright. Her lovely face filled with determination. After a long and solemn pause, she said, "I will help you, Atuk."
>
> "Would you? Honest?"
>
> To prove it she stepped right up to him, her eyes squeezed shut against anticipated distaste, and kissed him on the mouth. "It's the very first time for me," she said.
>
> "I'm so afraid," Atuk said, his voice quivering, "of failing."
>
> Bette kissed him again, forcing his mouth open. When she was done, Atuk cleared his throat and poured himself a rather strong gin and carrot juice.
>
> "Aren't you even . . . don't you feel . . .?"
>
> "It's no use," he said.
>
> Bette pulled him down to the rug with her and led his hand to her breast. "This should be very stimulating for you," she said. She kissed him even more passionately, rolled over on him, tried a couple of other sure-fire things, and then pulled back to look at him quizzically.
>
> "Well," he said, "I do feel a certain . . . "
>
> "Good."
>
> "I think my pulse-beat *has* quickened."
>
> "That's progress, isn't it?"
>
> But it seemed to Atuk there was a sour edge to her voice now.
>
> "That's all for tonight," she said.
>
> At the door, however, she suddenly clung to him.
>
> "I hope you realize," she said, "that no man has ever even held me in his arms before. I couldn't you see. Because I belong to the nation. Like Jasper Park or Niagara Falls."

This ingenious, amoral Atuk is the same scheming, materialistic Atuk who attempts to mass-produce Eskimo art as demand for it increases. He brings his relatives from Baffin, imprisons them in a basement, and sets them to work. Their reward is Atuk's "magic," by which he pretends to produce pictures from the television set. Unfortunately, his scheme backfires. His realtives begin to make their sculptures look like the models on television. Atuk is enraged. He is not angry at the decline of their native culture. He is angry because they are not producing what the customers want:

> Atuk had a look at the day's output. Every painting was representative. Literal. The statues were perfectly shaped. All crudeness and innocence gone. "For Christ's sake," Atuk said, ripping a painting in two, "if I want Norman Rockwell quality goods I can hire Rockwell."
>
> Brothers, sisters, cousins, aunts and uncles, all tried to conceal themselves behind the thrusting, bellicose figure of Ignak.
>
> "I should have guessed you were behind this. Well, speak up."
>
> "Why is it," Ignak asked, "you always want us to paint and sculpt badly?"
>
> "That's what they want, not me."

Comically and with refreshing gusto, the character of Atuk is laid bare. He is no *ingénu;* he is no innocent needing his naiveté to carry him through the mazes of a bewildering, sophisticated world. He has all of the qualities that the world to which he has come admires: a pretence of culture, unswerving ambition, and ebullient aggressiveness.

Richler's message is equally clear. This is not simply an anti-American novel, satirizing the dominance of New York over Toronto or the drowning of Canadian culture by American culture. It is a novel which attacks hypocrisy everywhere, the hypocrisy particularly that hides desire for fame and fortune behind the facade of sham culture. That is why Seymour Bone, Canada's Rudest Drama Critic, is pilloried so unmercifully. His fame as a critic had come to him quite accidentally. Before attending his first play for the *Standard,* he had eaten so much that, though he was enjoying the performance enormously, he was forced to leave before the end of the first act. The effect was as immediate as it is comical – he received a national reputation as a harsh critic:

> . . . Bone went to the theatre constipated and woke up a national figure. But his newly-won reputation was also to ruin his pleasure for years to come. For the truth was that Bone was delighted by most plays, specially if they were full of salty jokes or good-looking girls, but he felt that if he didn't walk out on every second one people would say he was going soft. So walk out he did, often returning in disguise the next night to surreptitiously enjoy the rest of the play.

Businessmen, academics, artists: none fares any better under the scorching examination of the novel. Everywhere the degeneration fostered by mass culture is laid bare. Rovere's contemptuous and startling words have the ring of truth: "Cut off from American junk, Canada would have to produce her own." Junk is the common currency.

Richler is not alone in his statement. Many commentators have made the same kind of declaration. David Karp, in his essay "TV Shows Are Not Supposed To Be Good," put the matter succinctly:

> Why is TV so bad and still so successful? Because American taste – and the taste of the English, French, Germans and other idiots – is awful. Lincoln is reputed to have remarked that God must have loved the common people, since He made so many of them. Lincoln must have made the remark when he was speaking as a politician. Politicians adore the common man and so does Proctor & Gamble. The commoner, the better. The saddening truth about television is that the audience is out there, listening, watching, in numbers which shake us and they haven't reached out to turn off their sets. They switch channels and the networks are as sensitive to the clicking of those switches as they are to the very air they breathe. But the sets stay on. More and more of them.

Richler sees the problem with an artist's eye. The result is an hilarious, pungent novel which is brilliantly conceived. It has not enjoyed the public or critical success of *St. Urbain's Horseman*, perhaps because the satire which is such an intrinsic part of the book is not always sustained successfully and because the writing does not always achieve the realistic flavour of the dialogue in *Duddy Kravitz*. However, it is an eminently worthwhile, interesting example of Richler's inventiveness.

St. Urbain's Horseman

This novel has received critical acclaim on both sides of the Atlantic. Some idea of the praise it has been accorded may be gathered from the *Time* cover story on Richler (May 31, 1971):

> . . . *St. Urbain's Horseman* may not be the Great Canadian novel, whatever that is. But it is, unquestionably, Mordecai Richler's best, and that is more than enough. *Horseman* amounts to a literary and personal stock-taking, a pulling-together of the various strengths that can be recognized in the author's earlier work. The result is a rich, complex, deftly controlled book, more self-revealing than anything Richler has done before and, above all, enormously funny.

For his central character, Richler returns to *The Apprenticeship of Duddy Kravitz* and selects Jacob Hersh. The choice is significant.

In *Duddy Kravitz,* Hersh is, above all, a reasonable, thoughtful and decent boy. He does not join in the tormenting of Mr. MacPherson, and he chastises Duddy for his tendency to make everything seem dirty. In contrast to Duddy, he is shown to be a good scholar. Moreover, he seems to be about to find himself as a person, for his decision to leave college and seek his future as a writer appears to be a rational, well-considered decision. Thus he offers a sharp contrast to the aggressive, bewildered and callous Duddy. To choose this figure as the hero, then, marks a decisive change in Richler's technique from the earlier novel.

The change is not only startling; it is both fitting and necessary. Through the figure of Jacob Hersh, Richler wishes to examine yet another aspect of alienation in *St. Urbain's Horseman.* The problem on this occasion is the problem of the exile: Jacob Hersh is a Montreal Jew who has made his home in England. In this situation, to make him an antihero, that is someone who is not basically likeable, would be to complicate his situation unnecessarily and also to restrict the ability of the reader to apply that situation and its problems to different circumstances.

Consequently, Jacob Hersh is, first of all, a decent, likeable person. For example, like most people of his kind, he has romantic fantasies about titillating self-indulgence, but when he actually has the opportunity to participate in a real orgy, his real nature asserts itself:

> . . . Suppressing nausea, Jake broke free, slid into his trousers, and sat down on a stool by the bar. He drank slowly, his head throbbing, as on the floor below they continued to thrash, roll, and writhe. Kiss, suck, gobble, penetrate. What is it with me? If I saw this in a how-empty-is-the-life-of-the-rich movie or read it in a lowdown-on-suburbia novel, I'd burn with envy, but now that it's happening to me – Jake scooped up a bottle of champagne and stepped on the terrace to watch the sun come up. The Mediterranean sun. Spain. Grubby fishing boats were beginning to chug into the harbour. Gulls swooped hungrily overhead or bobbed on the shimmering green water alongside. Remember this, Jake thought, cherish it, and he felt very ghetto-liberated, very Hemingway, as he raised a bottle to his lips, drained it, and flung it into the sea. A moment later he was sick to his stomach.

Jake cannot participate eagerly and freely in an orgy; he is repelled by the less-than-human activities involved. He cannot even be a flamboyant Hemingway hero, for his grand gesture in draining the bottle is followed by a very ordinary, human consequence: he is sick. Further, unlike Duddy Kravitz, Jake has no obvious problems to beset him; he has achieved a good measure of financial success as a film and television producer, and he is happily married.

Jakes problem is metaphysical. In his thirties, he is feeling acutely the purposelessness of existence which, he feels, belongs to his generation:

> . . . Young too late, old too soon was, as Jake had come to understand it, the plaintive story of his American generation. Conceived in the depression, but never to taste its bitterness firsthand, they had actually contrived to sail through the Spanish Civil War, World War II, the holocaust Hiroshima, the Israeli War of Independence, McCarthyism, Korea, and, latterly, Vietnam and the drug culture, with impunity. Always the wrong age. Ever observers, never participants. The whirlwind elsewhere.

"Ever observers, never participants" is the key phrase. Thus his generation had never been called upon to grapple directly with the horrors into which they had been born; their parents had fought that battle. And yet they were not untouched by the horrors. This is what distinguished them from the younger generation, who knew nothing at all of the horrors. Therefore, though his generation had not suffered, it was nonetheless haunted by the ghosts of suffering. Consequently, it had neither the powerful confidence of the older generation which had survived the suffering, nor the aggressiveness of the younger generation to whom suffering was unknown. His generation was trapped:

> As it seemed to Jake that his generation was now being squeezed between two raging and carnivorous ones, the old and resentful have-everythings and the young know-nothings, the insurance brokers defending themselves against the fire-raisers, it followed inevitably that, once having stumbled, he would be judged by one when accused by the other.

From this perception derives his anxiety. That anxiety has nothing to do with the financial worry that Duddy experienced. It has little or no relation to the minor guilt feelings that Duddy knew as he sought to achieve his materialistic destiny. The anxiety springs from metaphysical concern. It is indeed a tormenting sense of man's fragility in the universe, and is thus not aroused by the petty worries of day-to-day existence. The awesome sense of man's smallness can prompt various responses, of course. For the psalmist of the Old Testament, it is a source of wonder and rapture that his God should so have blessed his seemingly insignificant creation, and he cries out in astonished praise:

> When I look at thy heavens, the work of
>   thy fingers,
>   the moon and the stars which thou hast
>   established;
> what is man that thou art mindful of
>   him,
>   and the son of man that thou dost care
>   for him?
> Yet thou haste made him little less than
>   God,
>   and dost crown him with glory and
>   honour.
> Thou hast given him dominion over the
>   works of thy hands;
>   thou hast put all things under his
>   feet,
> all sheep and oxen,
>   and also the beasts of the field,
> the birds of the air, and the fish of the
>   sea,
> whatever passes along the paths of the sea.
> O Lord, our Lord,
>   how majestic is thy name in all the earth!

(Psalm 8 Revised Standard Version)

But to the man who does not have such faith in unchanging decrees and enduring absolutes, the perception of man's fragility in the universe is not a source of wonder and praise; it is a source of spiritual anxiety. For it throws man back upon his own resources. However, when the resources are weak, when man, for example, is seen to be the propagator of virulent corruption and horrifying evil, then the prospect is bleak indeed and the comfort absent.

The anxiety reveals itself everywhere in Jake's life. It is aroused most vividly by one event which is the core of the novel's plot. Jake has to stand trial, with the corrupt pornographer Harry Stein, on a sex charge. It does not matter that the victim was a willing accomplice or that Jake had not really committed the offences with which he is charged. What does matter is that, for him, the charge and the resulting trial are clear evidence of the threats to his existence that he had long waited for. The world had revealed itself in all its capriciousness. The battle was now in the open:

> What he couldn't satisfactorily explain to Nancy was that he was more
> exhilarated than depressed by the trial because at last the issues had
> been joined. Joined, after a fashion. From the beginning, he had
> expected the outer, brutalized world to intrude on their little one,

inflated with love but ultimately self-serving and cocooned by money.
The times were depraved. Tenderness in one house, he had come to
fear, was no more possible, without corruption, than socialism in a
single country. And so, from the earliest, halcyon days with Nancy,
he had expected the coming of the vandals. Above all, the injustice-
collectors.

The view of the world here is quite clear. On the basis of this
concept, the world is corrupt. Injustice is everywhere. The situation,
it is felt, cannot last long. Sooner or later, the crimes of man will
catch up with him and retribution will be exacted. The central figure
of retribution in the novel is St. Urbains Horseman, who is actually
Jake's cousin, Joey Hersh. It does not matter that actually Joey
seems to be a petty criminal who lives by his wits in many parts of
the world. For Jake, the mysterious, shadowy figure of his childhood
becomes the avenging Horseman who seeks for retribution everywhere. With apocalyptic fury, he will avenge the injustices visited
upon the emaciated millions of India, the starvelings of Africa, the
oppressed of the Western world, and, above all, upon the Jews of
Europe. Thus, Jake has a terrifying sense of man's injustice to man.
At times, the canvas of Jake's imagination shows the enormous
injustices, as in the picture of the concentration camps:

> The bodies are not lying scattered here and there throughout the
> room, but piled in a mass to the ceiling. This is explained by the fact
> that the gas first inundates the lower layers of air and rises but slowly
> to the ceiling. That forces them to trample and clamber over one
> another. At the bottom of the pile are the babies, children, women
> and aged; at the top, the strongest. Their bodies, which bear numer-
> ous scratches occasioned by the struggle which set them against one
> another, are often intertwined. The noses and mouths are bleeding,
> the faces bloated and blue.

At other times, the canvas is small, noting the pathetic ways in
which human beings struggle against their fate and seek to face
disaster cheerfully. In this category would be the many newspaper
items which Jake has observed. One is from "the page with the
human touch":

CHIN UP! THE POLIO GIRL CAN COOK

For 15 years Betty Ward has wanted to cook her own meals. And
in her iron lung she has read cookery books in the hope that one
day her dream would come true.
  Now with the aid of one of the latest pieces of apparatus for polio
victims she can cook at her home in Esher, Surrey. A remote control
unit has been fitted in her iron lung and it controls a hot plate and
a frying pan. She gives instructions to her mother about mixing the

ingredients and then controls the cooking by moving a switch in different positions with her chin.

"My most successful dishes," said Betty, "are pancakes and braised chops."

Another is the report of an interview with filmstar William Powell, a cancer victim:

"I began bleeding from the rectum in March 1938," he said. "The doctor found a cancer, smaller than the nail of your little finger, between three and four inches up my rectum. They recommended removal of the rectum. Then I'd have to have a colostomy and evacuate into a pouch through an artificial opening for the rest of my life. I didn't feel I could go for this. But the doctor said that for my particular case they could offer an alternative – a temporary colostomy and radiation treatment. I took it."

Surgeons made an incision in Powell's abdomen, brought out part of the colon, and cut it half through. "From then on," said Powell, "fecal matter emptied into a pouch round my middle." . . . Few cases of rectal cancer are detected early enough to be treated as Powell's case was. Says Powell simply: "I was one of the lucky ones."

Great or small, however, universal or individual, the sufferings and the injustices are clearly discerned. Society may seek to hide them behind a facade of cheery optimism or attempt to ignore them entirely, but the truth was clear: "The Gods raise you, only the better to strike you down."

Thus, in spite of his material success and in spite of his happiness with Nancy, Jake cannot be contented. He never does find contentment. The trial does not emerge as the critical battle he had imagined. Jake is merely fined five hundred pounds, while the friendless Harry Stein receives a prison sentence of seven years. The metaphysical issue, then, is unresolved. Symbolically, the trial has not settled anything. Further, Jake receives the news of Joey's death. He had died in an air crash while smuggling cigarettes. Jake becomes the Horseman:

In his nightmare, he was the Horseman now. It was Jake who was St. Urbain's rider on the white stallion. Come to extract the gold fillings from the triangular cleft between Mengele's upper front teeth with pliers. Slowly, he thought, coming abruptly awake in a sweat. "I've come," Jake proclaimed aloud.

Nevertheless, the ending is not without hope. True, the Horseman still seems to ride; true, Stein is seeking his own vengeance. However, Jake still has Nancy, who has stood by his side throughout his troubles. She has loved him; she has borne his children; she has comforted and guarded him in his depression; and she receives his love after the trial. Warm, affectionate, sexual, maternal, she is almost an earth-mother figure in her persistence in keeping life going. Perhaps it is through her that we are intended to glimpse the warm tenacity that features in human existence; perhaps in her is the theme of hope that Richler announces in his epigraph:

> Defenceless under the night
> Our world in stuper lies;
> Yet, dotted everywhere,
> Ironic points of light
> Flash out wherever the Just
> Exchange their messages:
> May I, composed like them
> Of Eros and of dust,
> Beleaguered by the same
> Negation and despair,
> Show an affirming flame.

W. H. AUDEN

Symbolically perhaps, the marriage of Jake and Nancy is the union that produces the "affirming flame," uniting as it does the "beleaguered" Jake and his metaphysical visions, and the warmly human Nancy.

The theme, then, is not small or trivial. That is why *St. Urbain's Horseman* may well be Richler's most effective novel to date. For he has obviously begun a task far larger than that involved in *The Apprenticeship of Duddy Kravitz.* In the early novel, the view was horizontal. That is, the author was looking *around* at the society which had spawned Duddy, and his analysis and observation remained, largely but not completely, on the sociological aspects. With *St. Urbain's Horseman,* Richler attempts to probe *inwards.* The novel is still a work which scrutinizes society meticulously, but, more important, it is also the mirror of a mind and the vehicle for a soul's expression. The weaving of fact and fantasy, the merging of dream and reality, the blending of memory and event – all give it a dimension larger than that of *Duddy Kravitz,* because they explore the shadowy regions that are the birthplace of guilt and that are the origin of men's archetypes.

This novel, then, is a more impressive work than *Duddy Kravitz.* The shrewd handling of the complex narrative technique, the maturer thrust of the satiric elements and the human seriousness of theme mark it as a work which deserves to be read carefully.

REVIEW QUESTIONS

1. Explain carefully the influences exercised upon Duddy by the following members of his family:
    - a. his mother
    - b. his father
    - c. his grandfather
    - d. his uncle

2. Write a character sketch of *both* Mr. Calder *and* Mr. Cohen. Describe and explain the similarities and contrasts between them.

3. Describe fully *either* Cuckoo Kaplan *or* Mr. Friar, and analyze the portrait for its revelation of Richler's technique in creating comic characters.

4. Write a character sketch of the Boy Wonder. Explain clearly his contribution to the novel as a whole.

5. Is Duddy one person or two? Discuss, using specific references to the novel in your answer.

6. Discuss *The Apprenticeship of Duddy Kravitz* as an exploration of the innocence/experience theme in literature.

7. "*The Apprenticeship of Duddy Kravitz* is more than simply an attack on materialism in society." Discuss the validity of this judgement, explaining carefully other themes which you find to be important in the novel.

8. Describe in detail the setting of the novel, explaining significant details relevant to the theme.

9. Write an essay in which you explain the structure of the novel.

10. Examine the appearances of Duddy Kravitz in *St. Urbain's Horseman*. Discuss his similarity to, or difference from, the Duddy whom we encounter in *The Apprenticeship of Duddy Kravitz*.

11. Describe some of Richler's satirical targets in the novel, explaining the characteristics that he is attacking.

12. Describe in detail one humorous scene in the novel, analyzing it carefully for the techniques employed.

13. Is *Duddy Kravitz* merely an interesting Canadian novel, or is it a work which deserves wider reading? Discuss.

BIBLIOGRAPHY

Articles About or By Mordecai Richler

BOWERING, George,   "And the Sun Goes Down," *Canadian Literature* #29, Summer 1966.

CAMERON, Donald,   "Don Mordecai and the hardhats," *The Canadian Forum,* March 1972.

NEW, William H.,   "The Apprenticeship of Discovery," *Canadian Literature* #29, Summer 1966.

RICHLER, Mordecai,   "The Uncertain World," *Canadian Literature* #41, Summer 1969.

TALLMAN, Warren,   "Beyond Camelot," *Canadian Literature* #4, Autumn 1969.

THOMAS, Audrey,   "An Offwhite Horse," *Canadian Literature* #51, Winter 1972.

WOODCOCK, George,   "The Wheel of Exile," *The Tamarack Review* #58, 1971.

The reader should also note the cover story in *Time* magazine, May 31, 1971.

Reference Books

PACEY, Desmond,   *Creative Writing in Canada.* Toronto: The Ryerson Press, 1967, First Paperback Edition.

WOODCOCK, George,   *Mordecai Richler.* Toronto: McClelland & Stewart, 1971, (Canadian Writers, Number 6).